Decolonizing the Curriculum through Theory and Practice

Marie Charles & Bill Boyle

"When you really know who you are, you wouldn't want to be anybody else" (Kamene, 2019)

All rights reserved. No part of this book may be reproduced or transmitted in any form or by any means, electronic or mechanical, including photocopying, recording or any information storage and retrieval system without written permission from the author, except for inclusion of brief quotations in a review.

Copyright 2020 by Marie Charles and Bill Boyle. All Rights Reserved.

Every effort was made to contact each author for permission to use the illustrations in this book

MFIT Copyright © (2016)
Many Faces In Teaching
McKelly Books
mcharles380@aol.com

Many Faces In Teaching

Contents

Published by: McKelly Books: 44 Pall Mall, Liverpool, UK

Contact Dr. M. Charles yellowaugust@hotmail.com
Contact Professor B. Boyle William.boyle1405@btinternet.com

Introduction

'Who am I?
Where in the world am I?
How in the world did I get here?' [Hilliard 1985]

These three fundamental tenets should supply the grounding to all conceptualization and design of a curriculum globally. Any curriculum should support an investigation of 'self' as that 'self' relates to regional and global history. Surely, the aim is to demonstrate the cultural unity and inter-connectedness of the human family.

This book needed writing because it is surely time to finally put to bed the tired, over-used narrative of why the starting point of black identity is positioned around slavery, servitude and domination? The context of that narrative can be situated across the range from the formulaic slave trade-based school 'history lesson in Black History Month' to the print-based or visual media debating forum.

Why, then, must that narrative be addressed? 'Because it is a systematic negation of the other person and a furious determination to deny the other person all attributes of humanity, colonialism forces the people it dominates to ask themselves the question constantly: 'in reality, who am I?' [Fanon, 1967, p.200]. The history books that the authors [as representatives of state school students in the mid to late 20th century] were exposed to in their own schooling journey majored on the triumphs, conquests and global expansion of the British Empire builders. The term 'colonialism' could equally be attributed to all the European countries who built 'empires' in other countries' territories. So, what has changed? Why in recent years has there been an upsurge of criticism of the colonial crimes of the past? The authors in this book attempt both to answer this question and to build upon the legacy of those inclusive schooling initiatives, which struggled against a dominant culture to engage and empower. Africana phenomenology [see Chapter 1] will recur regularly throughout this book positioned within Afrocentricity as a paradigm shift and as the methodological tool used by the authors to decolonize the curriculum.

The research described and analyzed in this book has its roots in the authors' previous work. Seminal to that research is the 'How Can only 18 black teachers working in Liverpool [UK] represent a diverse teaching workforce?' published report [Boyle & Charles 2016]. The consensus of the interviews from that research study evidenced that black[1] learners

---

[1] The word 'black' is erroneously viewed within a paradigm of connotative linguistics that positions oneself outside of the human family (Tariq Bey 2015; El Adwo, 2004). The Kemites (Egyptians) had only one term to

designate themselves **KMT = Black**.

This is the strongest term existing in the Nesut Biti/Pharonic tongue to indicate Blackness. This word is the etymological origin of the well known root Kemit (Obadele Kambon, 2019). Additionally, the term black here, is used throughout denotatively as a scientific term as proposed by Moore (2002) "That the physiological origin of blackness or pigmentation is a result of melanocyte functioning. Since melanin is associated with the distribution of numerous types of cells to other destination sites in the body, it is apparent that there is a critical role for the *darkness* provided by melanin (p.23-24). In Barr, Saloma & Buchele's 139 page Medical Hypothesis paper entitled: *Melanin: The Organizing Molecule;* It (blackness) functions as the major organizing molecule in living systems" (p.1). Dr Richard King (1993) provides a useful example: "If you can understand are being disempowered by the schooling system and that they do not see themselves within the curriculum. 'Through cultural reproduction and cultural in-group behaviour, it was further evident that the institutional actors, such as the teachers, classroom assistants and senior leaders have a dominant role in the perpetuation of the myth of African-Caribbean inferiority' [Charles 2019, p.2]. This triggered further research into whether critical pedagogies using a reframed learner-centred approach could offer new points of identification to empower diverse learners? The authors align firmly with the researched opinions of Hilliard and colleagues [1990] in positing that the history of Africans and African Americans in public schools and Higher Education is deficient in six areas. Reviewing these six areas, as follows, demonstrates that the deficiencies that Hilliard identified over twenty five years ago are still there today:

'1. There is no significant history of Africans in most academic disciplines before the slave trade.

2. There is virtually no 'people' history. The history of African people is presented, if at all, in episodes and figments of post-slavery.

3. There is virtually no history of Africans in the African diaspora. Students do not get a sense that the descendants of African people are scattered all over the globe.

4. There is presentation of the cultural unity among Africans and the descendants of Africans in the African diaspora.

5. There is generally little to no history of the resistance of African people to the domination of Africans through slavery, colonization and segregation apartheid.

6. The history of African people that is presented in mainstream curricula fails to explain the common origin and elements in the systems of oppression that African people have experienced, especially during the last 400 years.'

[Hilliard, Payton-Stewart & Williams, 1990, p.xx-xxi].

In response to Hilliard's evidence, Shockley [2008] offered three policy recommendations as follows:

1. Include African-centred theories and philosophies as part of pre-service teacher training programmes.
2. Incorporate [Akoto & Akoto, 1999] three phases of re-Africanization as part of the education of students, especially within schools where African Americans predominate.
3. At the local or district level, charge schools with the task of providing an education for Black children that incorporates information and knowledge on the following imperatives: [a] their African identity, [b] Pan-Africanism; [c] African cultures and

---

plant photosynthesis then you can understand human photosynthesis because chlorophyll is to the plant, as melanin is to the human- chloroplast cell is to the plant as melanocyte is to the human". Therefore, throughout this discussion, the words black, melanated and Melanated Global Majority (MGM) within this paradigm will be used interchangeably.

value systems; [d] Black nationalism; [e] Community control/institution building; [f] Educating as opposed to 'schooling' Black students [Shockley 2008].

As formative pedagogists [Boyle & Charles 2013; Charles & Boyle 2014], the authors' research and personal teaching experiences have lead them to investigate a model of human [student] empowerment based on an integration of formative teaching and learning [critical pedagogies], Africana phenomenology and Afrocentricity [see Figure 1 below]. The primary conceptual and theoretical framework for this study is Afrocentricity and Africana phenomenology situated within a critical pedagogical lens. These multiple lenses facilitated an understanding of how change in social and learning behaviour can occur as a result of increased understanding of learners' affective, conative and cognitive domains.

Framed within a pathway to praxis, the newly conceptualized teaching programme of Reframed Units of Change-RUoCs (Charles 2019) presented an evidenced gateway to a black identity rooted in cultural and historical achievements. The goal of this study, through intent and content, was to address the diminution of black learner voice and learner behaviours and consequently to raise the black learners' status as subjects with agency and power. The book's aim is in reducing bias in educational settings (institutions whose traditionally adopted anti-racist strategies are recognized in this study as narrow and ineffectual) and is founded upon formative pedagogical approaches. Its basis is a need to acknowledge how culture nurtures the psyche and that such anti-racist approaches must respond to well constructed multimodal teaching methodologies which are the foundation of the re-conceptualized model which are called Reframed Units of Change [within the curriculum]. This research, evidences that a multi-centric approach, to teaching, learning and most importantly identity; will challenge and prove positive against currently dominant forms of knowledge.

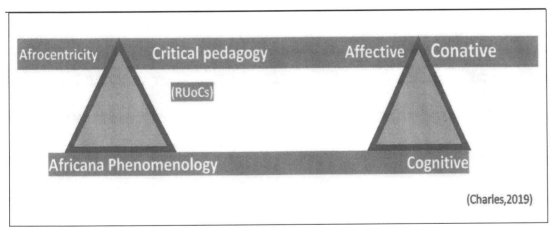

Figure 1: Model of paradigm shift (Charles, 2019)

Put simply, this conceptual model, which is based on a paradigm shift which places the learner at the centre of the teaching and learning process, enables the learner to look at the world through his/her own eyes [lens]. Previously the learner has been an 'outsider' to the curriculum and its content, which has been taught in the classroom. The educator/teacher needs to start from an understanding that the learner will not make learning progress without the student's affective domain. Thus, motivation enthusiasm, self-esteem, interest, sense of well-being; must be integrated with that student's conative and cognitive domains [i.e., the self-driven act of putting the increased 'interest level' of the student's affective domain into practice, the praxis] [Charles & Boyle, 2014, p.81]. This book demonstrates to the reader how this inclusive learning model is expressed through demonstrations of student engagement while experiencing within normal classroom teaching sessions based on the author's Reframed Units of Change [RUoCs]. Those reframed Units form the basis of a teaching programme, which is adaptable for all age ranges.

All curricula should spiral around and embrace a form of integration with the humanities subjects. Therefore, when the student is studying mathematics or science, those subject domains should reflect what the student is learning in the social sciences. For example, Iamblichus describes Pythagoras' years as a student among the Egyptian priests with these words "…he frequented all the Temples with the greatest diligence and most studious research…he passed twenty two years in the sanctuaries studying astronomy and geometry" (Poe 1997, p.101). When the geographer Strabo toured Egypt in the first century BC, he was shown the places where Plato and the Greek mathematician Eudoxos had lived and studied while under the tutelage of Egyptian priests' (ibid p.109). These examples indicate the necessary integration of mathematics, geography, science and history.

This is a book with both practical and policy messages across the range of educational stakeholders. Its intended audience, is all those involved in the teaching and learning process. Academics and university teachers and lecturers, school leadership, managers and curriculum planners, teachers and parents, teacher training organizations and suppliers of professional development support for teachers, national educational policy makers, those education system stakeholder groups who all hopefully embrace the understanding that the learner is at the centre of any national and/or international curriculum planning and centre-periphery programme. Our book's focus is on explicating and modelling the teaching of a reframed, decolonized curriculum as a means of promoting effective learning in an inclusive schooling environment. The authors use multimodalities and multiliteracies [language, print, images, graphics, gesture, sound & movement] as the core pedagogical approach for teachers and exemplify the use of these resources for learners [Charles & Boyle 2014]. To enable this, the author conceptualized and designed and developed a series of reframed curriculum-based teaching Units. The initial five Units have been piloted under research fieldwork conditions as follows: **Genesis of Geometry; People & Places; Measurement: Order & Arrangement; Artefacts as Evidence; Language & Etymology of First World People. Each of the five Units is sub-divided in strands of teaching and learning activities.**

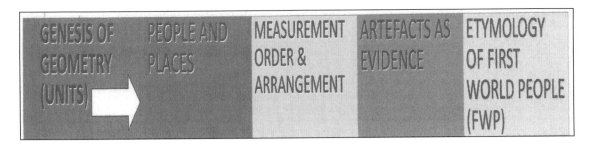

Figure 2: The five Reframed Units of Change

The book concentrates on the teaching sessions for the themes in the first of those Reframed Units, the *Genesis of Geometry*. Using the evidence of the teaching and learning interactions and the dialogue of and with the learners from the piloting of those teaching sessions, each of the Chapters of this book follows the structure of:
identifying and setting out the conceptualization and planning of the teaching theme and its relationship to the overall reframed curriculum unit. The teaching resources and the formative 'guided group' teaching approach. Transcripts from the teaching and learning interactions and dialogue; followed by a summary of the teaching session.

The author 'tracked' a sample of fifteen children and each theme-related chapter describes the small group ['guided group' formative pedagogy] teaching and learning sessions, evidence and analysis of the sample children's involvement in learning, their learning behaviours and their development as empowered learners.

The **Genesis of Geometry** Unit is sub-divided into the following five strands of teaching and learning activities [as detailed in Figure 3 below]. **Global connections & triangles; Squaring numbers and their historical origins; Physics and concentric circles; Concentric circles, people and pyramids; Etymology: the roots of history through words, place names and peoples.**

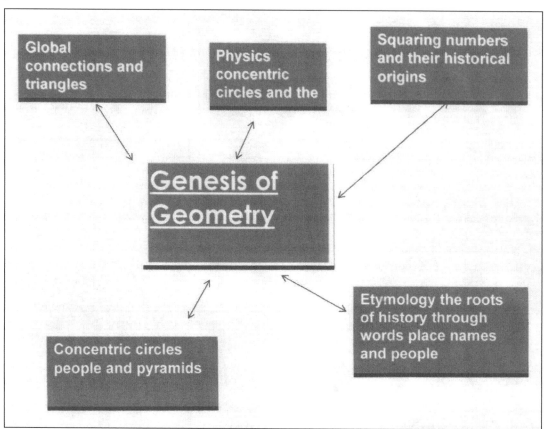

Figure 3: Genesis of geometry taught sessions

The Chapters of the book explore these teaching sessions. The book concludes with a Chapter on the Black Genesis of Geometry and a Conclusion, which draws together and analyses how the Reframed Units of Change within the curriculum support the development of learner identities, learner potential and learner empowerment.

The research in this is book challenges the colonization of the current taught curriculum and its Eurocentric paradigm. The authors use the evidence from their own research [Boyle & Charles, 2010; Boyle & Charles 2016; Charles, 2019] to address and challenge the absence of diversity and the consequent distortion of history as the current models offered to students in the schooling system globally. Through engaging systematically with a critical pedagogy and modeling a pathway into praxis, this outlined the dominant approach in the classroom.

The primary conceptual and theoretical framework for this book is Africana phenomenology situated within a critical pedagogical lens, which is necessitated by its irreconcilability with a Eurocentric paradigm. These multiple lenses of phenomenology and pedagogy are situated within Afrocentricity. Afrocentricity forces the reader into a consideration of an alternative global perspective. This theoretical framework enables an understanding of how changes in social and learning behaviours can occur as a result of educators' increased understanding of learners' affective, conative and cognitive domains – and the importance of the positive integration of those domains in the learning empowerment of all students in all phases of education. In the current profile, the dominance of Eurocentrism takes up all the space.

Framed within a pathway to praxis, the research based re-conceptualized teaching programme of Reframed Units of Change (RUoCs) presents an evidenced gateway to an empowered student identity rooted in cultural and historical achievements. The authors' aim throughout is to critique and challenge the current curriculum's episodic format and its misleading historical chronology which has and is restricting learner voice and learner behaviours. 'Being locked into a 5,000 year old biblical time frame' [Valentine, 2018]. This challenge and change, then, will raise for learners their status as subjects with agency and power rather than constrain them to remain as objects of analysis, identified only as dehumanized, fixed points as under-achievers on norm-referenced data-driven performance league tables. For example, the Rhind Mathematical Papyrus is often considered as the best existing example of ancient Kemetic Mathematics. Its modern name comes from Alexander Henry Rhind, the Scottish antiquities collector who purchased it in 1858 in Luxor. The Rhind Mathematical Papyrus proves to us that our Kemetic ancestors invented algebra. Unfortunately, the scribe Ahmes receives no credit for this act [Osaze, 2016, p.40].

For the research fieldwork, which supplied the data for this book, the specific teaching materials from the Reframed Units of Change that were taught to reinforce an empowered black identity within the human family, were the five teaching sessions of the Genesis of Geometry (**see Figure 3 above**). The author, in authentic teaching sessions, analyzed the dynamics of race, culture and learner identity of fifteen children from mixed ethnicities with whom she worked with over a seven month period in a primary school in the north-west of Britain. The author, as a formative teacher, observed how the children responded to the empowering, learner-centred classroom culture in the sessions, the intent and the content of the teaching and resource material. Higher order, formative skills such as self-regulation, learner autonomy and goal oriented behaviours were observed. Through cultural reproduction and cultural within-group behaviour, it was further evident that the institutional actors such as the teachers, classroom assistants and senior leaders have a dominant role in framing and modeling the 'ideal learner' and in the perpetuation of inferiority for 'othered' learners.

The book's principal aim is to promote inclusion for all learners through providing a model of inclusive teaching which will support the reduction of bias in programmes of pre-service and in-service training for all teachers. These pre-service programmes and subsequent in-service continuous professional development experiences are based on formative teaching and an understanding of the 'what', 'why', 'when' and 'how' of teaching [and subsequently developing their own modules of] a de-colonized curriculum which, over time, will become the framework of a universal 'taught curriculum'.

The authors' approach is founded upon inclusive, empowering, multimodal, formative, pedagogical approaches [Boyle & Charles 2013, Charles & Boyle 2014]. The basic tenet of the book is the need to understand, acknowledge and then address how culture nurtures or, in specific environments, negates the psyche of the student. It is a basic concept of teaching and learning surely that a 'nurturing pedagogy' is present in all educational settings and is continuously offered within the learned experiences of all students - and for that to happen in our classrooms and seminar rooms, requires well constructed multimodal, formative approaches. That is the philosophy at the foundation of this book's Reframed Units of Change. The research at the core of Chapters 3 – 7 and the consequent pedagogical methods detailed and evidenced in this book model a multi-centric approach to teaching, learning and identity with the aim of challenging and offering positive alternatives to the currently accepted dominant forms of knowledge. Identity is paramount in a positive educational journey for a learner. Consider the words of Dr Chike Akua [2012; 2019]: 'If regular identity theft is where someone steals your personal information to gain access to your resources and wealth, *Cultural Identity Theft* is when someone steals your story. How do you take the people who gave the world: reading, writing, language, literature, architecture, mathematics, sciences, medicine and technology? How do you take that group of people and convince them that they are nothing but a race of pimps, players, criminals and thugs?' [p.71]

Chapter 1: Historical context: setting the scene

'There I was, challenging this sea of whiteness' (Yancy 2004 p.3)

In 2014, University College, London (UCL) students initiated a campaign called: *Why is My Curriculum White?* These students were campaigning against the general range of educational stakeholders' ''lack of awareness that the curriculum is white comprised of 'white ideas' by 'white authors' and is a result of colonialism that has normalized whiteness and made blackness invisible" (Peters, 2015, p.641). The authors throughout this book emphasise that 'Whiteness' is both cultural and a social concept. 'Whiteness' can also be viewed as a racial perspective or a world view. This perspective shapes the interactions and paradigms of its individual members. This world-view allows 'Whiteness to be defined as 'normal' and gives 'Whiteness' a sense of privilege 'Whiteness' and Blackness' were invented as antipodes within the context of English and, later, American slavery (Leonardo, 2002, p31). Blackness became [and too frequently remains still in a common perception] associated with bondage, inferiority and social death. As stated in 'Whiteness with freedom, superiority and life' (Desmond and Emirbayer, 2009 p.338).

Almost congruent with the UCL initiative, an interrogation of the United Kingdom's Department for Education [DFE] reported GCSE performance data (over a ten-year period, 2004-2014) in Strand, (2015) evidences the socio-political outcomes which created the data for UCL's movement to address. The under-achievement of black Caribbean children [as represented through those data] produced a narrative in the media of those children's perceived inability to perform and to succeed as learners. Schooling, within its socio-political dimensions related to educational institutions, is a major site of social and cultural reproduction according to sociologists Bourdieu,
[1986/2011] and Bowles & Gintis [1976]. As recently as 2009, Carroll is commenting that "the culture of dominant groups forms the knowledge and skills that are most highly valued and forms the basis of what is taught in schools" (2009, p.37). Therefore, curriculum and forms of pedagogy are central instruments in the transmission of cultural and social reproduction. Peters (2015) argues: "this kind of reproduction takes place through misinterpretations of history and the 'othering' of [people], shaping subjectivities and identities" (p.643).

The author addressed this issue in this book through her conceptualizing, designing, writing and trialling in schools, a five-unit programme. As outlined in the Introduction to this book, the individual units are: *Genesis of Geometry; People & Places; Measurement: Order & Arrangement; Artefacts as Evidence; Language & Etymology of First World People.* All these modules are intended to be taught as a whole, in which the subject domains of language, mathematics, history, geography, science, arts and music are integrated within an affective, nurturing, formative pedagogy.

The prevailing narrative of damaged histories and the subsequent mythologizing of black people as intellectually and culturally inferior can be traced back to the birth of a belief system facilitated by "the hierarchizing of differentiated racial categories" (Outlaw, 1996, p.173). Burrell (2010) traces the origin of this myth of black inferiority to colonialism and states: "It is as though the original colonial elites hired a PR agency to sell the concept that Africans were innately inferior... and the last several centuries still haunt black advancement and achievement" (p.xiii). For Barthes (1977), "Myths serve the ideological function of naturalization. Their function is to naturalize - to make dominant cultural and historical values, attitudes and beliefs seem entirely 'natural', 'normal', self-evident, timeless, common sense and thus, objective and true reflections of the 'way things are' (p.45-46). This narrative over time developed its own hegemonic effect and the resultant diminution was not challenged for centuries.

A 1684 publication by Francois Bernier: 'A New Division of the Earth' is considered by academic researchers to be the first published post-classical classification of humans into distinct races. His racial taxonomy proposed that there were four or five types of races. Carl Linnaeus (1707-1778), who was considered the father of anthropology, also claimed that there were four basic races, namely: "Europaeus Albus (white European), Americanus rubescens (red American), Asiaticus fuscus (brown Asian) and Africanus Niger (black African), (in Loring Brace, 2007, p.27).

To compound his norming categorizations, Linnaeus created a "wastebasket taxonomy; monstrous for wild and monstrous humans, unknown groups, and more or less abnormal people" (Willoughby, 2007,p 33-34). The leading racial theorist of late eighteenth-century Europe was the German born physician Johann Friedrick Blumenbach (1752-1840) who devised the colour system and argued that 'the Caucasian had been the 'original racial form of mankind, of which the four later types were degenerations' (in Kidd, 2007,p 9). Degruy (2015) argues that the classification of races was the birth of pseudo-scientific racism, which was void of any scientific basis, and was the precursor to DNA methodology, in particular mitochondrial DNA (mtDNA) application. Wesling (1991) proposed, in an important distinction with regard to inferiority and genes, that 'functional inferiorization' is a social process first, that negatively enacts upon genetic potential in ethnically diverse students.

The development of the academic fields of Black psychology has ushered in a new respect for the legitimacy of various ethnic conceptions of psychological functioning. In fact, Black psychology has forced the overall field of psychology to recognize that there is no universal psychiatric reality, and in terms of psychological knowledge and practice, the only valid perspective is one that reflects the culture of the people served (Nobles, 2015, p.33).
.

Relative to the above, Nobles' view that "European contact with Africa has always been driven by a desire to transform or rearrange African phenomena into fundamental European constructs in the service of domination and exploitation" (2015,p.37) could be seen as a necessary, if not overdue, twenty first century starting point of addressing such overt racism. Furthermore, in the process of 'being, becoming and belonging' (Nobles, 2015, p.13), should we as practitioners be asking ourselves: 'What are the psychological effects of inculcating damaged histories on the minds of ethnically diverse groups and on their emerging learner identities?'

The triangulated aspects of culture, history, and personality have been recognized more acutely by Wilson (1993): as "psychohistory, the psychological result of undergoing certain historical experiences" (p.20). He argues that: "We must recognize the intimate relationship between culture, history and personality. If we do not know our history then we do not know our personality. And if the only history we know is other people's history then our personality has been created by that history" (p.23).

In keeping with an historical context, and in parallel to the birth of racial classifications, was the rise of human expansion across the globe through exploration and exploitation. The polygenetic theory of evolution propagated the belief that humans were separate and distinct races; this was central to upholding the ideology of inequalities and hierarchies in intellectual capacity. This was propagated by a proliferation of fakes and forgeries such as the discovery of the Piltdown skull found in 1912 by amateur anthropologist Charles Dawson. However, in November 1953, *Time* magazine published evidence gathered by anthropologist Kenneth Page Oakley; paleon-anthropologist sir Wilfred Le Gros Clark and Joseph Weiner that the Piltdown skull was a forgery. The monogenetic theory is that all modern humans stem from a single group of Homo sapiens. Homo sapiens emigrated from Africa 40,000-60,000 years ago and spread throughout the continents (Budge 1907; Chancellor Williams 1987; Clarke, 1993; Diop 1974; Dixon 1923; Gaillard & Reid 2014; Gibbons 2009; Hom 2015; Obenga, 1995, 2004; Scheinfeldt et al, 2010; Van Sertima 1995).

The archaeological, linguistic, anthropological, historical and cultural evidence is simply overwhelming for an African genesis of civilization. However, Diop (1974) argued that: "Our investigations have convinced us that the West has not been calm enough and objective enough to teach history correctly, without crude falsifications" (p.xiv). Diop's statement raised a fundamental issue: 'History is not just an episode; it is the unfolding of the human family on planet earth and in the cosmos (Jefferies, 2015 in Nobles 2015, p.12). In support of this episteme, the United Nations Declaration on Race and Racial Prejudice (1978) states:

'All human beings belong to a single species and share a common origin. They are born equal in dignity and rights and all form an integral part of humanity. All peoples of the world possess equal faculties for attaining the highest level in intellectual, technical, social, economic, cultural and political development. The differences between the achievements of the different people are entirely attributable to geographical, historical, political, economic, social and cultural factors. Such differences can in no case, serve as a pretext for any rank ordered classification of nations or peoples' (Objective 1, p 60, emphasis added).

In consideration of this, and the question posed earlier why is the dominant narrative in schools globally positioned around the teaching of slavery, domination and colonialism from a Eurocentric viewpoint? Additionally, perhaps a deeper, more pressing area of enquiry should focus on: "European contact with Africa has always been driven by a desire to transform or rearrange African phenomena into fundamental European constructs in the service of domination and exploitation" Also, in the process of 'being, becoming and belonging' (ibid,p.13), should we as practitioners be asking ourselves: ' What are the psychological effects of inculcating damaged histories on the minds of black children and on their emerging learner identities?'

The National Association of Black Psychologists celebrated its fiftieth anniversary in June 2018. Its very recent inception and infancy can be viewed in contestation to Western psychology which has traditionally been held as omnipotent, privileging and universal. Psychologist Wade Nobles proposes: 'The development of the academic fields of Black psychology have ushered in a new respect for the legitimacy of various ethnic conceptions of psychological functioning. In fact, Black psychology has forced the overall field of psychology to recognize that there is no universal psychiatric reality, and in terms of psychological knowledge and practice, the only valid perspective is one that reflects the culture of the people served' (2015,p.33).

In summary, the empowering potential of presenting truthful historical, cultural and pedagogical content needs to be introduced to our students and be positively and iteratively disseminated into our schooling spaces.

There is a need for the potential positive outcomes of presenting truthful, historical, cultural and pedagogical content to be illustrated and evidenced to our students and be disseminated into our schooling spaces. Du Bois (1903) recognized the importance of not only understanding history in relation to one's identity and psychological formation but equally, our constant connection to history as past and present:
'We can only understand the present by continually referring to and studying the past. When any one of the intricate phenomena of our daily life puzzles us; when there arise political problems, race problems we must always remember that while their solution lies in the present, their cause and their explanation lie in the past.' (in Turner, 1984, p.167).

An important step in understanding and responding to the work of Nobles (2015), Wilson (1993) and Du Bois (1903) is in the necessary dual action of the reclamation of history and of self. The following thoughts on 'Africana Phenomenology' [see Figure 4 below] is an attempt to restore 'the missing pages of history' (Clarke, 1993); and "start with the bold assertion that Africa is the basis of world history... black scholars must be courageous enough to make this assertion and prove it academically" (Turner, 2014, p.33).

Figure 4: Africana Phenomenology in Paget (2006)

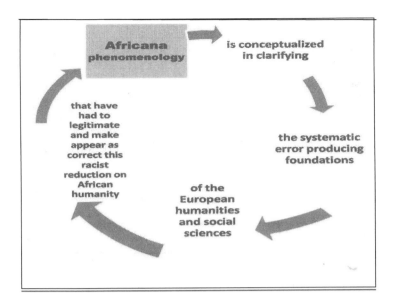

Figure contents:

Africana phenomenology → is conceptualized in clarifying → the systematic error producing foundations → of the European humanities and social sciences → that have had to legitimate and make appear as correct this racist reduction on African humanity →

"The early Africans believed that the first impulse of the One is to realize *consciousness*" (Asante, 2000, p.17 original emphasis). 'Seeking the Sakhu' as the process of 'knowing of oneself' was conducted by "the dwellers of the Nile valley who ushered in the dawning of human consciousness" The central upper facade of every temple in ancient Kemet had a carved winged orb to signal the origination and activation of the sacred tenet 'Know Thy Self' (Mfundishi, 2016; Finch, 1998;)

Embree (1997), identified seven approaches to phenomenology namely, descriptive (transcendental); naturalistic, existential, generative, genetic, hermeneutic and realistic (in Chan, Fung & Chien 2013, p.1). The purpose of selecting a descriptive, transcendental, qualitative phenomenological method in the exploration, interaction and teaching of the researcher's programme: RUoC to Key Stage Two children is to explore: "The lived human experiences and the way things are perceived and appear to the consciousness" (Tuffour, 2017, p.2). Simply put, how human beings perceive, understand and live in the world is the subject matter of phenomenological study (Bullington, 2013, p.20).

Phenomenological inquiry as proposed by Husserl is a method of investigating the nature of existence. It is therefore, emic and idiographic (1931, p 2). This critical aspect, that Tuffour (2017) raises embraces the significance of the study of internal cultural elements (socio-cultural domain), alongside the personal, private self that is produced in its distinct and unique way. This complex relationship requires a front and centre recognition of the individual. This fundamental component cannot be underplayed or sidelined within the definition of phenomenology. In short, the self is everything. Joyce & Sills (2014) discuss a series of skills that researchers are required to master within this domain: "Bracketing is an attempt to identify and acknowledge the preconceptions, judgements and attitudes that the researcher inevitably carries into the research relationship" (pp.16-17). The requirement to suspend all judgement finds itself consistently stated in phenomenological research literature; (Gearing, 2004; Chan, Fung, & Chien, 2013). However, realistically, how is this mode of thinking to be fully operationalized, if we, as human beings are socially and culturally mediated? Indeed, sociologist Jeanne LeVasseur suggests that bracketing is highly problematic and has been historically undertaken as a technique to indicate scientific rigour, however, we must employ "fresh interpretations of bracketing" (2003, p.408). Similarly, Joyce & Sills (2014) offer a way forward: 'Bracketing is not about attempting to be *free* from preconceptions, attitudes or reactions. It is an attempt to keep close to the newness of the here-and-now moment and avoid the danger of making hasty or premature judgements about the meaning of each participant's unique experience' (p.17, original emphasis,).[2]

The congruence and compatibility which connect the strands of a formative pedagogy, an Afrocentric episteme and phenomenological inquiry, are observed and commented upon by social theorist Patricia Hill Collins (1989). Similarly, Houston & Davis (2002) suggest that "both frameworks treat 'co-researchers' (as opposed to mere objects) as experts of their life experiences" (p.124). In this regard, "personal experience or the consciousness that emerges from personal participation in events is considered as solid evidence" (Foss & Foss, 1994, p.39). Indeed, "phenomenology contends that personal expressiveness and emotion are central (as are logic and reason) to knowledge, theory and research" (Houston & Davis, 2002, p.125).

This qualitative method, in the context of the phenomenon under study, clearly majors on the individual and the distinct, unique consciousness that emerges from and within a cultural space. Therefore, an added inevitable series of questions emerge: How then does the researcher reconcile the utilization of phenomenology from its colonial and Eurocentric dominance? How does the researcher rescue the closing down of the intellectual potentialities of *'what it is to be'* within any learning space? Finally, why is it that this interrogative probing is either actively resisted or simply ignored? The necessary dialectical and geographical 'rescuing' as one of many steps, that Paget (2006) urges phenomenology to enact, has already commenced from the opening lines of this section. Indeed, Lewis Gordon, a professor and philosopher of human sciences and phenomenology, contends; "Phenomenology is the most viable method for postcolonial liberatory thought and struggles' (Nissim-Sabat, 2008, p167). Gordon emphasises in his book *Disciplinary Decadence* (2006*)* that: "We treat our discipline as though it was never born and always existed and will never die. Thus, if one's discipline has foreclosed the question of its *scope*, all that is left is a form of 'applied' work...that mitigates against thinking" (Gordon, 2006, original italic emphasis pp 4-5).

Gordon (ibid) is implicitly requesting us as researchers to actively interrogate the methods within our chosen disciplines because these methods are not set in stone, and as they are human made, they cannot possibly cast a wide enough net for all research cases and contexts. His provocative use of 'decadence' as a dominant signifier intimates the presence of 'decay' in the academy, as he demands that serious scholars 'surpass those impositions

---

[2] consciousness- *'con'* with, thoroughly; *'scient'* knowledge (Kamene 2018). *'Scient'* skilful; knowing (Merriam-Webster, (1828),= 'with thorough knowledge')

of decay with generous offerings of living thought" (p.11). Gordon is also probing and challenging our acceptance of universalism and the 'crisis of knowledge'. He asserts that this 'crisis of knowledge' has come about because of a 'war on reality'. This is because of "the failure to garner and use the evidence of lived experience that gives the lie to certain influential and far reaching assertions" (2006, p.2). He writes that "the war on thinking has led to a situation in which ideas have become increasingly divorced from reality" (2006, p.32). His critique supports the work of political sociologist and cultural theorist, Paget Henry (2006) who asserts that: 'Africana phenomenology has been forced to exist in the non-rational, and a-theoretical shadow, cast over it by Western philosophy in general and Western phenomenology in particular' (p.1).

Tuffour (2017) signalled (see above) the importance of emic and idiographic domains within phenomenology. Therefore, as Paget (2006) and Gordon (2006) argue, 'that any countering or refutation of hegemonic disciplinary dominance will inevitably result in a 'crisis of knowledge'. Put simply, researchers are faced with direct issues of what is theoretically 'in' and what is theoretically 'out'; therefore, the constant task requires the: "unshackling of the colonial relationship of the African as experience, for white theoretical reflection demands much ontological and epistemological resistance' (Gordon, 2006, p.79). In 1944 John Dewey took a similar stance in his classic *Democracy and Education*: 'To say that they are 'disciplinary' has safeguarded them from all inquiry. It has not been enough to show they were of no use in life or that they did not really contribute to the cultivation of *self*' (1944, p.133, emphasis added). In this statement, Dewey (1944) is overtly criticizing the taken for granted, omnipotent assumptions of knowledge-producing practices and the crucial relationship of the human being within this process. Gordon (2006) calls this a 'special kind of decay'.

In utilizing a phenomenological approach, it is traditional and somewhat customary to adopt the works of Husserl (1887), Hegel (1807) and Heidegger (1914), as these most authoritative ethnological European thinkers of the discipline asserted a strong cultural particularity, which placed Africa and peoples of African descent at the bottom of the scale of humanity. Consider Georg Wilhelm Friedrich Hegel's philosophical phenomenology as follows: 'It is characteristic of the blacks that their consciousness has not yet arrived at the intuition of any objectivity...He (the black man) is a being in the rough' (trans. Nisbet, 1975, p.138). Hegel stated that the Negro was completely sensual: "To the sensual Negro, human flesh is but an object of sense-mere flesh" (trans Nisbet, 1991 p.95). Curry (2017) argues that for Hegel "the savage Negro was trapped in the natural condition of being" (p.43). Gordon (2006) constructs his critique of Hegel by stating: "The result of the Hegelian thesis was much ignoring of medieval African thought and the complex intellectual history of various African nations well into the mid-twentieth century" (p.70).
Therefore, if, as Hegel (1910) asserts, that 'self-consciousness is a social phenomenon' and that one can only know oneself in relation to others i.e. "self-consciousness exists for another self-consciousness...it is only by being acknowledged or recognized" (p.229). Then, this has profound implications for how black bodies engender external perceptions, and as a result, how those perceptions are internalised. In brief, "Hegelian phenomenology-is over

dependent on the others' conscious awareness of one's existence" (Taylor, 2007, p.8). Consequently, what if one cannot see oneself through one's own eyes? These outcomes are clear for Gordon (2007), 'The dialectics of recognition, that follow, all collapse into subordination, into living and seeing the self only through the standards and points of view of others. Without their recognition, one simply does not exist (p.125).

The process of socialization argues that 'reality' is socially constructed (James & James, 2008). However, for Nichols (2018) this 'truth' has nothing to do with 'reality' and that socialization itself imprints 'isms' of all different kinds. This phenomenon has been thoroughly theorised by two influential figures from the tradition of African phenomenology; W.E.B. Du Bois (1903/1965) and Frantz Fanon's (1967) humanizing phenomenology. Du Bois (1965) articulates in his *Souls of Black Folk* that: 'A world, which yields him no true self-consciousness; but only lets him see himself through the revelation of the other world...of measuring one's soul by the tape of a world that looks on in amused contempt and pity' (p.215).

For Du Bois, this negation of an accurate formulation of the completeness of black self-consciousness is always tied to an asymmetrical relationship - directly and indirectly to whiteness. This fact, for Du Bois, results in a lack of subjectivity and the fragmentation of self. Du Bois's phenomenology, as observed by Henry (2006), was intricately linked to an ethical/practical project that tirelessly fought to reclaim the full recognition of the humanity of Africana peoples. Henry (2006) argues that this included the 'de-niggerization of Africana identities" (p.8). Indeed, professor of gender and race studies, Arthur Saint-Aubin asserts: "the dominant culture needs its niggers, its ugly inferior, its 'other' to construct itself as superior and beautiful (1994, p.1058). In Du Bois's (1898b) classic text *The Study of the Negro Problems,* he articulates the danger of pathologising black people outside of a social critique in which 'the negro is viewed as *the* problem' as 'We ordinarily speak of the Negro[3] problem as though it were one unchanged question, students must recognize the obvious fact that this problem, like others, has had a long historical development. Moreover, that it is not *one* problem, but rather a plexus of social problems...and these problems have their bond of unity in the act that they group themselves about those Africans whom two centuries of slave-trading brought into the land' (1898b, p.3 original emphasis). And on the issue of black inclusion: 'The widespread conviction...that no persons of Negro descent should become constituent members of the social body (Du Bois, ibid ,p.8).

In order to counter these socio-cultural and ontological tensions, the Du Boisian phenomenological development of 'second sight' or, as Henry (2006) terms it, 'potentiated second sight', is an attempt to locate squarely, the influence of a European hegemony on

---

[3] The Negro: A "blackface" stereotype and the categoric form of self-blindness and deformation that the white mind was constantly producing and projecting (Henry, 2006, p.8). The etymological roots of Negro: 'blackness', 'darkness', 'death'; negro-subhuman chattel/cattle; necro/nekro = corpse-a divination by calling up the dead (George William Lemon, 1783, pp 336-337)

Africana self-consciousness. Du Bois (1965) wrote that 'the negro was gifted with second sight' (p.215) which is born from a socialization process that inculcates the role and recognition of others' to form one's self-consciousness (Hegel, 1910). Henry (2006) argues that this second sight "is the ability of the racialized Africana subject to see him/herself as a 'negro', that is, through the eyes of the white other with no real true self-consciousness" (p.8). Is Du Bois's use of the word 'gift' to suggest, that this was an unwanted 'gift', that one could return because it was faulty and damaged? Or through active resistance, would take the individual on a journey back to 'first sight' which is the ability to see one's self through one's own eyes. This, is the true 'gift' of Du Bois's phenomenology [see Figure 5 below] , the idea that one must always seek out, nurture, and activate: "The cultivation of such an 'I' which would then become either a new form of first sight or some new form of third sight" (Henry, 2006, p.9).

This gift of consciousness is already bestowed by and on the African through *'Know Thy Self'* in Nile valley civilization (Mfundishi, 2016; Hilliard, 2003; Barashango, 1989,1991; Kamene,. 2017) and significantly opened up this chapter. However, what if my reality, which, in forming my self- consciousness as truth, is based, on an entry point of black identity that is centered on slavery, colonialism and servitude? How do I put back together a fractured self-consciousness in an educational setting that negates the affective, conative and cognitive domains of black learner identities? Finally, what is my reality as truth, if teachers are socializers of a second sight phenomenon?

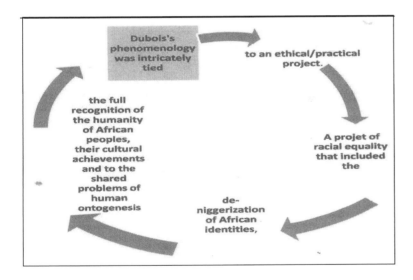

Figure 5: Dubois' Phenomenology in Paget, (2006)

Psychologist, philosopher and writer Franz Fanon[4] (1975) in his classic text *Peau noire, masques blancs* (Black Skin, White Masks) develops further the Du Boisian phenomenology as an extended conceptualization as *'being-for-others'* (p.89). In that text

---

[4] Fanon's original title of the book was: Essay of the Dis-alienation of the Black. Stuart Hall (1995) in Frantz Fanon: Black Skin White Mask. A film by Isaac Julien & Mark Nash.

he describes himself as a Negro but "naturally I don't know that because that is what I am" (p.155). Fanon's *'being-for-others'* is his articulation of an external imposition on psychic identity; this identity is then based on locating the external physical body as colour and phenotypic appearance, which merge to represent purported internal characteristics: 'The external form of this state is the substituting of an epidermal identity in the place of a cultural one. The inner content of this outer transformation is the socio-historical reality of being forced to live as the unconscious, liminal shadow, the repressed and undesirable side of the imperial European subject that had racialized its identity as white' (Henry, 2006, p.12).

Fanon (1975) describes an episode in which he is sitting in a train carriage when a child turns to her mother and says "Tiens un negre"- 'Look a negro' (p.90). In his chapter: *The Fact of Blackness* Fanon's racial epidermal schema triggers the 'historico-racial schema': "Dirty nigger! Or simply, "Look a Negro!" (1967, p.82). The child in the train carriage did not speak to him or ask him any questions; he was simply now the recipient of a 'white gaze' that had shown him in his thorough condition of *being-for-others*. Macey (1999) prompts the reader to look more closely at what the child exclaims and what is revealed in those three simple words: "Why the child in fact sees a *negre* and not a man with a scar on his face? (Fanon had a highly visible scar on his left cheek). How does the child know who and what it is seeing?" (p.9). Weate (2009), provides a deeper analysis of the train episode as an ontological violation, viewed as dramatic, because the gaze is from a child: "racist attitudes in Europe have permeated to the level of the *innocent'* (p.8, original emphasis). 'Racial epidermalization' is seeped within the culture and operates from all angles and functions, according to Zolatova (2009), like a panopticon; keeping the black person under constant inspection" (p.2). Fanon (1967) extends Du Bois's double consciousness into triple consciousness or third-person, in order to explain his encounter on the train; he is now no longer occupying his lived body in real time as he is outside of his body occupying his racial epidermal schema. "Look a negro!" words that are all-embracing in undifferentiated code and asymmetrical trajectory, as the child could have said 'Look a monkey' with the same effect of objectification. "And then I found that I was an object in the midst of other objects" (Fanon, 1967, p.82). Taylor (2007). suggests that Fanon's "movement and recognition to the white world is not returned in a reciprocal fashion" (p.83). Simply put, what could he say in response to the white child, which would have had equal force, meaning, and veracity? More pointedly, and culturally, why would there be a need in the first place to utter such a label to a stranger? Indeed, Fanon (1967), states that he is in a "zone of non-being" (p.82). In other words, Henry (2006), argues that for Fanon this encounter with the white other was experienced as an "amputation, an excision, a haemorrhage" (p 14). 'Her gaze is not a simple seeing, an act of direct perception, but a racial production of the visible, the workings of racial constraints on what it means to "see" '(Butler, 1993, p.16). Philosopher George Yancy (2014) suggests that Fanon is describing a process in which he is having his body phenomenologically returned to him. This paradigm for Yancy extends into what he frames as 'The elevator scenario'; another powerful phenomenology or lived reality of black bodies, which he captures in his chapter *White Gazes:* 'In terms of the elevator effect, I exist ontologically quadrupled. I appear to be in four places. For example, I am "here", taking up space outside the elevator before its arrival. I am also "ahead of myself". In other words, "being-ahead-of-myself" suggests the sense in which I am always already *fixed, complete, given* - in short; *I am placed before*. Before I enter the elevator, I exist in the form of a static racial template. My 'being' is known by whites before my arrival. I reside in a fixed place, always already waiting for me. Once on the elevator, though physically separated from the white woman, I am "over there", floating as a phantasm in her imaginary, a kind of thought bubble. Yet, I am also "alongside" myself as "here-ahead-of-myself-over-there-alongside-myself". It is an experience; that forces me to ask about the whereabouts of my body (2014, p.58, original emphasis).

In this outline of his thinking, Yancy (2014) is describing the elevator scene as both literal and microcosmic in the sense of greater and more "dynamic processes of a larger, systemic form of colonial invasion" (ibid) are at play. Yancy is forcing the reader to acknowledge, at least, two issues. Firstly, the power of culture and history on the shaping of identities through Fanon's (1967) epidermal racial schema in which, "the other... who had woven me out of a thousand details, anecdotes, [and] stories"(2014, p.84); creates a paradigm in which, 'my being is known by whites before my arrival'. Secondly, Yancy (2014) signals the importance of embodiment in relation to perception and the meanings that different phenotypic bodies carry into the world. In essence, "race" is lived and experienced, through the body both individually and generally as our bodies" (Mahendran, 2007, p.194). To experience 'being in the world' (corporeal existence) is to platform the importance of not only discursive language but equally, one's ability to see, feel, touch and describe situations. Merleau-Ponty's (1962, 1968, 2002) *Phenomenology of Perception* is an important contribution to' being in the world', as he centralized the body in relation to our interactions within our environment: "My body is a movement towards the world, and the world my body's point of support" (2002, p.408). What if the reader was to supplant Yancy's (2014) 'elevator scenario' for the spaces within our schools and classrooms in which black children reside? Have their bodies already arrived 'fixed, complete and given?' In doing so, do they exist; 'as a static racial template'? The volume of research strongly suggests that the answer is 'yes '(Wright & Counsell, 2018; Howard 2008; Ladson-Billings, 2011; Goff et al. 2014; Ferguson 2000; John, 2005; Kunjufu, 1984,1986,1990), and indicate that those stereotypes include being lazy, aggressive, and that "black children require a tough hand to keep them in line" (Emdin, 2016, p.5). In this context, the notion that 'race is only a social construction', coupled with, the 'I don't see colour' paradigm. is highly problematic as it suggests, as argued by Yancy (2014), that this "White talk, is another way of avoiding the *lived* reality of race. And the ways in which the rhetoric of white-colour blind antiracism; installs a problematic universalism" (p.50. original emphasis). Merleau-Ponty's (1968) phenomenology of embodiment as expressed in his book: *The Visible and the invisible* seeks to 'rescue each person for her unique perspective' as *possibilities of the same world*" (p.41 original emphasis). His respect and identification of each individual, is featured strongly in his work and contributions to the field. However, Mahendran (2007) points out that Merleau-Ponty never applied his theory to an interpretation of colonialism, and Merleau-Ponty's: "project was to establish a universal ontology irrespective of society, culture and institutions" (p.196).

In Merleau-Ponty's (2002), "the body schema is finally a way of stating that my body is in-the-world" (p.115), coupled with "*possibilities of the same world*", is his assertion that the body has free historical agency, which, argues Weate (2009), on the part of able-bodied beings is, false. Similarly, Mahendran states that: 'Fanon argues that if we take this normative corporeal schema and subject it to a history of anti-black racism and anti-black existence, Merleau-Ponty's universal corporeal schema loses some of its universal givens. In short, Fanon implicitly charges that Merleau-Ponty's theory of normative corporeal schema is therefore, based upon European man, a white man (2007, p.198). Merleau-Ponty's corporeal schema is both particularized and insular, and is therefore, limiting in its scope as it is unable to capture adequately, black experiences as raced and *his-storied* bodies.

Indeed, Fanon (1967) describes this lack of historical agency: 'Everything has been foreseen, discovered, proven, taken advantage of. My nervous hands rein in nothing; the vein is exhausted. Too late!' (p.91). Here, Fanon attempts to describe the absolute saturation, domination and utter control of the colonized knowledge of history. Are his words prophetic? To consider that, for example, in the 21st century schools are still teaching slavery as the entry point for black identity devoid of any black agency. The Maafa[5] is, as argued by Jefferies (2013), a European conceived, sustained and maintained phenomenon and that this level of analysis, is conspicuously absent in schools. Gordon (2007), Knies (2006) and Henry (2006) call for a new Africana phenomenology that has its roots in the "reinvention of the human in new revalorizing Fanonian terms (Nissim-Sabat, 2008, p.171) stating that, 'I want the world to recognize, with me, the open door of every consciousness. O my body, make me a man who always questions! (Fanon,1967, p181). Fanon's prolific output and influence on the issue of identity and knowledge of self as human being in the world forces the educationist to consider those three key questions:
'Who am I?
Where in the world am I?
How in the world did I get here?' [Hilliard 1985]

---

[5] The Maafa is a Kiswahili term for 'terrible occurrence' or 'great disaster'. It refers to the black holocaust when millions of Africans died during the journey of captivity from the west coast of Africa to the shores of America, and the Americas known as the Middle Passage. The word Maafa; was introduced by Marimba Ani's (1998) book: *Let the Circle be unbroken: The Implications of African Spirituality in the Diaspora.*

Chapter 2: The Importance of Culture

"To embrace one's culture is not to 'go back to the 1500s, it is not to reject technology. It is not to reject appropriate social and cultural change. It is not to reject categorically 'Western Civilization'. It is not to disrespect the culture of anyone. To embrace one's culture is to do merely what any healthy group does" (Hilliard, 1995, p.9).

There are many definitions of our understanding of culture and what the word means on both an individual level and in a collective basis. Hall (1976) suggests that "Culture is not genetically inherited, and cannot exist on its own, but is always shared by members of a society" (p.16). Hofstede (1980) defines culture as "the collective programming of the mind which distinguishes the members of one group from another" (pp.21-23). Lederach (1995) states that "culture is the shared knowledge and schemes created by a set of people for perceiving, interpreting, expressing, and responding to the social realities around them" (p.9). Therefore, culture, viewed from the definitional viewpoints of these theorists is a social process that one is born into as an existing order coupled with the negation of any genetic inheritability. However, recent work around epigenetic research as it relates to culture, by Galanter et al (2017) report in their study of a group of diverse Latino children in San Francisco that their DNA methylation (an 'annotation' of DNA), *altered* their gene expression without changing the genomic sequence itself. "The scientists claim that more understanding is needed in terms of how social, cultural and environmental factors interact with genetics to create differences in outcomes between different ethnic populations" (in Weiler 2017,p.1). Similarly, Loi, Savio & Stupka (2013) state: "Sensitivity to social structures, i.e. some epigenetic phenomena are highly responsive to environmental changes, which are affected by social institutions" (p.143).

In short, culture is a very powerful phenomenon. What if my epigenetic tags are intergenerational, unbroken negative experiences? For example, held beliefs which are then stated as, blacks were only slaves, or Europeans brought civilization to Africa, or Europeans were the progenitors of humanity. People, places and experiences then become the conduits to create the carriers of consciousness and self identity within the minds of young children. Therefore, if culture is viewed dichotomously and reduced to nature versus nurture as opposing entities i.e. translated into superior and inferior beings, this can result in the development of implicit bias/unconscious bias, stereotyping and deficit thinking in both limiting and restrictive ways.

This paradigm in a cultural setting has the potential to negatively affect "the collective programming of the mind which distinguishes the members of one group from another" (Hofstede, 1980, pp 21-23). Lee traces the role of this dualistic ideology within history of dividing ideas and matter into 'thinking things and non thinking things'. "This split or schism reflects the tradition from Plato and Descartes, which not only insists on the possibility of such separation, but also prioritizes ideas and thoughts" (2014, p.2) based on this cultural mindset. Rather than understanding the importance of complementarity and interrelatedness, and how these factors are always enacting and interacting with each other (Nobles, 2006; Carruthers,1999; Van Sertima, 1995; Hilliard,1995). Nothing happens in a vacuum. The implications of the aforementioned studies quite literally suggest that one's cultural environment can actually alter us genetically. This aspect is further complicated and exemplified through an exploration of socio-historical and cultural stereotypes, in which the labelling of fixed and growth mindsets (Dweck, 2006) has been applied to different ethnic groups in the classroom.

The model minority stereotype described by Lee (2009) "is a racist discourse which categorizes, evaluates, ranks and differentiates between groups; in which, for example, *All* Asian students are stereotyped as intelligent, studious and compliant" (p.165). Surely, then, this cannot be deemed as negative framing because to be considered intelligent and studious is very positive? As the highest achieving ethnic group in England's national examinations (for example, at GCSE [students age 16, in UK schools], based on UK government's Department for Education results for 2014/15; 2016/2017), the Chinese and Indian students have been described [by teachers as well as policy makers] as the model minority (Wong, 2015, p.733) and the ideal learner. However, a paradigm that operates within an essentialized and dichotomous way, such as 'black white', 'good/ bad', 'beautiful/ ugly', floor /ceiling (intelligent-unintelligent) binary system, creates what Gillborn (2008) describes as: 'The mere fact of minority success is positioned as if it automatically disproves the charge of racism against all minoritized groups; and in the UK, comparisons are made with 'underachieving groups' so that the latter are cast as deficient and even dangerous. Racists have always played favourites, viewing some groups as exotic mysterious and alluring, while others as bestial, savage and threatening. The same processes are at play in contemporary classrooms and staffrooms. The exceptionally high expectations that many teachers hold about Indian and Chinese students is the flip side of the same coin that involves the cultural demonization of black students' (pp.151 &153).

In 2017, the Department for Education ranked Black Caribbean and 'White and Black (so-called bi-racial) students as the lowest attaining ethnic group in achieving 5 A-C GCSE's nationally[6]. Gillborn (2008) presents a perceptive analysis of cultural embodiment in which the 'playing out' of raced bodies are stratified streamed and ranked for all to see in published league tables. However, the language that Gillborn (2008) uses to describe 'minority' and 'minoritized' is a deeply entrenched, semiotic, psychological illusion, woven into the cultural fabric.

Demographic statistics support this by weight of actual numbers. Drew, Sleek & Mikulak (2016) in a paper written for the Association for Psychological Science; report: 'When the Majority becomes the minority, the United Kingdom is on track to become the most ethnically mixed country in the Western world in fewer than 40 years. In fact, 'Whites' are *now a minority* in London, according to UK census figures' (p.2, original emphasis).

---

[6] In 2018, the UK government Department for Education changed the GCSE grading definitions from letters to numerics.

Similarly, in the United States of America, "by 2050, minorities would make up more that 50 per cent of the population and *become the majority* (original emphasis, p.1). Richeson, a psychologist, suggests that the prospect of losing majority status was likely to make people (perhaps unconsciously) uneasy (for example the influence of 'race' on the UK EU Referendum 2016). Which group of people is Richeson (2017, in Resnick, 2017) referring to as feeling uneasy?

Indeed, the power of language simply cannot be overstated, particularly in relation to its psychological effects on the formation of young children's identity and their world-view concepts. Consider that the etymon of the word 'minority' at its root means "less than" (Collins National Dictionary,1972, p 320). Ferguson (2014) presents similar definitions from the Merriam-Webster Collegiate Dictionary:

- A number or amount that is less than half of a total

- The group that is the smaller part of a larger group

- A group of people who are different from the larger group in a country, area, etc. (Merriam-Webster dictionary, p.1).

As long as we continue to use the term 'minority' as a synonym we are defining and consigning people to a lesser status and a less significant role, in short, ultimately, to powerlessness (Ferguson, 2014,p.2). Language has the power to influence our thoughts and actions; language has a deep psychological effect on how we see humanity and ourselves in relation to and within the world itself. Frances Cress Welsing (1991) recognized the pervasiveness of this reversed paradigm: 'In today's very small world at least three-quarters of the people are 'non-white', and the members of this 'non-white' majority population are subjected to domination throughout their lives, either directly or indirectly, by a tiny minority of the world's people who classify themselves as 'white' '(p.1). Furthermore, Buchanan's (2002) book *Death of the West* reports: 'Of the twenty nations with the lowest birth rates[7] in the world, eighteen are in Europe. The average fertility rate of European woman has fallen to 1.4 children, with 2.1 needed to replace the existing population. This does not mean ZPG (Zero Population Growth), this means ZP-Zero Population' (p.13).

However, Wesling's (1991) use of the term 'non-white' is also problematic as it serves to signify a base, a norm, a standard against which or within which all people must construct their identity. Otherwise, Wesling presents the very salient fact that unequivocally relates to

---

[7] In 2000, there were 17,400 fewer births in England and Wales than in 1999, a drop of almost 3 percent, and the lowest since statistics began to be kept in 1924 (Buchanan, 2002, p.19). The study on fertility, published in the Lancet, followed trends in every country from 1950 to 2017. Professor Murray reporting on the findings: "The fertility rate in Niger, West Africa is 7.1, but in the Mediterranean island of Cyprus women are having one child on average. In the UK, the rate is similar to most Western countries. More economically developed countries including most of Europe, the US, South Korea and Australia have lower fertility rates". Professor Murray (2018) concludes: "We will soon be transitioning to a point where societies are grappling with a declining population" (in Gallagher, 2018, pp. 2-3).

world-wide demographics as: "the use of language ultimately reveals the primary psychological dynamic" (p.5). Put simply, this indicates that our perceptions have been successfully altered in relation to factual 'minority' and 'majority' status. In other words, how is it that a small minority of people could rule over a majority people in South Africa, economically, politically and militarily? However, in 'real political' terms, Franz Fanon (1967) argued that racist structures are embedded in the psychology, economy and culture of the modern world. And that a "true culture cannot come to life under present conditions" (p.187). Former Chairman of the Commission for Racial Equality, Trevor Phillips relatively recently gave a speech in which he suggested that the phrases such as black and ethnic minority (BME) and, Black, Asian and Minority Ethnic (BAME) have become outdated, existing purely to: 'Tidy away the messy jumble of real human beings who share only one characteristic-that they don't have white skin... we could potentially adopt terms commonly used in the US such as 'visible minorities or 'people of colour (in Goodwin 2015,p.1).

Clearly, Phillips' nomenclature substitutions are still fraught with difficulty and are highly problematic, particularly, as many of these definitions are imposed from 'without' and supply merely a 'top down' mechanism of hegemonic origination. This raises the age-old agenda items of: Who holds the power to name and why? And whose agency is diminished? However, Phillips presents a cogent argument that strongly indicates and evidences the existing lack of understanding about complex heterogeneous groupings. The word 'Ethnic' according to Richardson (2006) in 'its use unhelpfully implies that 'white people all belong to a single group 'the majority', and that there are no significant differences amongst them. In point of fact, there are substantial differences within the 'white' population including ethnic differences... there is frequency an implication of exotic, primitive, unusual, non-standard... (p.6).
Richardson (2006) contends that "Language is both contested and continually changing as each generation establishes a way of speaking and this is challenged and overthrown by the next generation" (p1). Not only is this semiotic re-structuring healthy, natural and necessary; it also demands collegiate collaboration in order for the iterative aspects to continually unfold in a conducive climate. Cultural analyst Marimba Ani (1994) argues that ultimately the liberation of our thought from its colonized position will require the creation of a new language (p.10).

So, how, is this, then all related to culture? Classrooms are microcosms of society within a nation. Indeed, Riddle (2017), a senior lecturer of teacher education and early childhood, suggests that; "schools kind of work as a little microcosm of society and you can tell a lot about a society from its schools". However, Riddle (2017) cautions against the attack on teachers: 'The assumption that underlies all of this is we have a problem with teachers and schools but none of this addresses the material, social, economical, political and cultural inequalities that pre-exist when a student walks into a classroom' (in McGowan, 2017, p.3). Although Riddle's (2017) perspective seems helpful at first glance in relation to the array of influential factors involved, it is an attempt to 'remove' teachers from the very processes that he is describing and to distil the powerful impact of being socialized in a culture as described by researchers such as Hall (1976), Hofstede (1980) and Lederach (1995).The underlying premise here is to distance and dichotomize teachers, students and their environments as fragmented, superficial strands that are tied tentatively together. Somehow, the student is the 'carrier' of these pre-existing inequalities yet, paradoxically is not to blame. This semantic side-stepping ideology inevitably creates a line of thinking which inevitably leads to 'the student as deficit model'.

In (2009) the then Department for Children, Schools and Families (DCSF), of the United Kingdom government, released a document entitled *'Building Futures: Believing in Children: A focus on provision for Black children in the Early Years Foundation Stage'*. The front cover of the document reveals the dominance and consistency of this already hinted at dichotomous ideology. Stuart Hall's (1997) pre-dated comments on racialized regimes of representation signal this cultural need and obsession: "On racialized representational practices that reduce black children/populations to a few simple essential characteristics and deploy 'splitting' strategies to fix categories of difference in order to exclude or expel everything which does not fit" (p.247).

 Figure 6: Believing in Children DCSF (2009)

In this government document, there are in total fifty- five images of children – fifty of the images are exclusively of melanated children and only five images feature a 'white' child or 'white' adult. Culturally, what does this mean? For Barthes (1977) the signified (the black child) is generated through forms of myth-making mythologies: "Their function is to 'naturalize', in other words to make dominant cultural and historical values, attitudes and beliefs seem entirely 'natural', 'normal', 'self-evident', 'timeless', 'common sense' and thus, objective and true reflections of the 'way things are' (pp 45-6). Stuart Hall (1997) comments along the same lines of thought twenty years later that 'The voyeuristic gaze of the white reader gleans meaning through a long and deeply historicized practice of racial representation that stigmatizes and 'fixes' the supposed intellectual inferiority of the black child' (p.239). In the UK government's twenty first century exclusive presentation of black children as the only dominant images throughout the document, this places the children as objects of analysis outside of a socio-cultural framework. Therefore, "myths can serve to hide the ideological functions of signs and codes" (Chandler, 2002, p.145).

27

If school is a function of community and if school is a function of culture (Johnson, 2013), where did the 'white' children go? Where did the Asian children go? Where did the Chinese children go? Where did the Pakistani children go? Where did the Indian children go? And where did the 91% nationally 'white' teaching workforce go? [Boyle & Charles 2016]. These ritualized exclusions serve to maintain a social and symbolic order, rendered, according to Barthes (1977), as 'normal', 'common-sense' and 'the way things are'. Culturally, this is in keeping with the rules and the reader does not question the semiotic tensions that exist on the front cover of the document. Therefore, the 'problem' of black underachievement is placed squarely on the shoulders of the black child and the communities in which they live. Professor John (2012) reminds us that 'this deficit paradigm is so pervasive, as if white power structures and the policies that sustain them have absolutely nothing to do with the condition and experience of black students in the schooling system (p.5).

Analysis of the National Early Years Foundation Stage Profile (EYSFP) Teacher Assessments for 2015 data evidences that black heritage children are outperforming their Chinese, Asian, and on a par with, their white peers. However, this high level of performance soon becomes a regression as evidenced in GCSE scores (showing black pupils at the 'bottom'), a regression which begins and continues throughout the black child's taught experience on her/his journey through primary school. By the time the black child has reached secondary school, her/his motivation, sense of learner identity and self esteem has been so reduced that the enthusiastic 4 and 5 year old who outperformed her/his peers in Early Years is languishing 'on the floor' as the political metric describes failures. GCSE data from Liverpool schools evidences the black pupils are 10 percentage points under the 50% success rate for the 5 GSCE- A-C national standard, (DfE, 2017), a standard which is exceeded by the black child's Chinese, Asian, and white peers.

This is a reversal of the normal expected profile of an education system and demonstrates that the 'educational pipeline' (the student's journey from early years to employment or higher education) is not operating in an equitable manner for a black child. This is reinforced by Gillborn (2008) who argues that "the assessment game is rigged to such an extent that if black children succeed as a group despite the odds being stacked against them, it is likely that the rules will be changed to re-engineer failure" (p.91). His evidence, which tracked students by ethnic group from the age of 5 to the age of 16, is worth quoting in full: The data on all six Local Education Authorities (LEA) indicated that Black attainment fell relative to the LEA average as the children moved through school. The data on one LEA was especially striking: in the largest LEA in our sample (also one of the biggest authorities in the country) we found that Black children were the *highest* achieving of all groups in the baseline assessments...At age five Black children were significantly more likely to reach the required levels: 20% points above the local average. And at age 16, the end of compulsory schooling, the inequality was so bad that Black children were the *lowest* performing of all principal groups: 21% points below the average (Gillborn, 2008, p.99). Similarly, professor Gus John (2006) cites that 'The Government's own Social Exclusion Unit has acknowledged the research evidence that black students (Caribbean heritage boys in particular) outperform everybody else up to the age of 7, some sustaining that high level of performance up to the age of 11, but are among the worst under- performers by the age of 14 (p.27).

In a recent BBC (2016) programme titled: *Will Britain ever have a Black Prime Minister?* research by Burgess (2013) was cited to report the outcomes of test scores and subjective assessments within the school population in England. His analysis stated that 'When we take course GCSE's that are marked outside of the school... we looked at data comparing the test score of pupils in England against their teacher assessment, and for some ethnic[8] groups we found that the teachers systematically under-estimated their performance relative to how they did in these remotely marked tests. That, suggests to us that there is some stereotyping going on... that teachers have formed a view about the likely capabilities of students' outside knowledge that informs the expectations that they have of the students in the classroom. The stereotyped view might be that Black students are not very good in school, and so they tend to under assess them, have lower expectations for their attainment progress. These stereotypes interact with the child's motivation [BBC 2016].
However, in response to the programme's findings, former head teacher, school inspector and A level chief examiner, Mark Ellse (2016), stated that this was tantamount to stirring up resentment in ethnic groups and questioned: 'how much damage do we cause to that culture by erroneously suggesting that there is nothing they can do themselves to improve their lot, because they are oppressed by a system that is stacked against them'? (p.3). If Ellse is suggesting that there may be damaging consequences for black pupils in revealing 'the code' in all of its transparency, then evidence indicates that he may be correct. Moreover, is Ellse inadvertently admitting that there is inherent bias in the system and furthermore, that these black pupils need to be aware of this bias to address this disempowerment? Ellse fails to acknowledge the tremendous power and influence that teachers have over their students throughout the schooling experience. Sociologist, professor Boliver from Durham University stated: 'Whether you want to call it unconscious bias or institutional racism, let's acknowledge there's a problem and make it better, being defensive on this issue is getting us nowhere' (In Harewood, 2016, p 4). Indeed, open, honest and pointed dialogue which is proactive and solution oriented is a preferable move in the right direction.

According to Young (2016) implicit biases take the form of subtle, sometimes subconscious stereotypes held by the individual (p.2). No-one is immune to implicit biases; they are both pervasive and robust (Greenwald, McGee & Schwartz, 1998; Kang, et al 2012; Nosek, et al, 2007). Even people, with avowed commitment to impartiality and fairness are susceptible to these unconscious biases (Rachlinski, Johnson, Wistrich & Guthrie, 2009). It is also important to recognize that "teachers from the same 'racial' group as their students do not have a 'built-in' capacity to be excellent teachers of those students" (Nieto, 2002,

---

[8] Stuart Hall (1992): "I am familiar with all of the dangers of 'ethnicity' as a concept and have written myself about the fact that ethnicity, in the form of a culturally constructed sense of Englishness and a particularly closed, exclusive and regressive form of English national identity, is one of the core characteristics of British racism today" (p.256).

p.231).The notion of 'racial matching' is criticized by Goldenberg (2014) who suggests: 'it is inaccurate to automatically assume a teacher's race completely qualifies or disqualifies him or her from being an effective teacher. However, Goldenberg continues by stating that: "the overwhelming number of white teachers in non-white classrooms is problematic" (p.118). Research by Gilliam (2016), showed 135 educators' videos of children (aged 4-5 years old) in a classroom setting. Each video had a black boy and girl and a white boy and girl. The teachers were told the following: we are interested in learning about how teachers detect challenging behaviour in the classroom. Sometimes this involves seeing behaviour before it becomes problematic, while the teachers were asked to detect 'challenging behaviour', no such behaviour was apparent in any of the videos. Yet when asked which children required the most attention, 42% of the teachers identified the black boy (p.11). This research is interesting on two fronts: firstly, the team of researchers used eye-tracking technology to capture each teacher's physical movement in the surveillance of each child; secondly, their findings support previous research in which "Black boys were found to prompt a less essential conception of childhood than their White same-age peers, and that black boys are under closer scrutiny in the classroom' (Goff, 2014, p.526). These findings traverse physical and geographical spaces/countries and underline that globally the black population share a cultural set of educational experiences that are unique.

The situation described in Bernard Coard's (1971) work: *How the West Indian Child is made educationally sub-normal in the British school system,* has remained unchanged in the last five decades. His work described an education system which placed a disproportionate number of 'West Indian' children in Educationally Sub-Normal schools [ESN] following IQ tests which sustained cultural and class bias, maintaining a status quo and preserving a hegemonic social hierarchy. The anti-banding or streaming campaign (1969-1970) formed by the Black Education Movement and the Black Supplementary Schools Movement (1968-75) campaigned against proposals by Haringey Council to 'band' or 'stream' black pupils in the Borough's schools. The Doulton Report (1969) revealed the following: On rough calculation about half the immigrants will be West Indians at 7 of the 11 schools, the significance of this being the general recognition that their I.Q.s work out below their English contemporaries. Thus, academic standards will be lower in schools where they form a large group. (Haringey Comprehensive Schools' Section 5 (c) 13 Jan 1969, in George Padmore Institute Archive Catalogue).

Two decades prior to The Doulton Report (1969), a similar study: *Colour and Class in Six Liverpool Schools (*1950) published by the University of Liverpool, echoed the same belief that 'Coloured' students were intellectually inferior. Furthermore, the study claimed that this was based on "classifying the children into two kinds of groups, white and coloured, and having superior and inferior clothing" (p.23). The study concluded: "The results show that there are a larger number of outcasts in the coloured population in the Local Authority Schools; it also shows that there are significantly more children who are outcasts in the inferior clothing group" (p.41). The children had also been grouped scholastically by their clothing into 'superior clothing' (groups A & B) and those with 'inferior clothing' (groups C & D) p.17.

In a 2005 interview Bernard Coard stressed the importance of understanding schooling practices within a wider, socio-cultural-historical context. He raised the importance of recognizing that: 'The lesson to be learned for today's problems in the school system is that they were 'hatched' decades ago in the previous two generations. When society fails one generation of children, it lays the foundations for similar, even worse failures to follow. We human beings inherit not only our genes, but often also from our social circumstances.' (p.2).

Brittain's (1976) research supports the same argument, namely, that teachers hold stereotypical views of MGM students. Based on a postal questionnaire of a sample of 510 teachers in primary and secondary schools in the UK, Brittain's data analysis found that two-thirds of teachers reported West Indian children as having low ability and being a discipline problem (p.182).

Wright (1992) conducted an ethnographic study of four multi-racial inner-city schools: A total of 970 classroom observations with 57 staff, support staff, and head teachers, 38 interviews with parents and an analysis of test results in three schools. Wright found that the vast majority of staff ...seemed genuinely committed to ideals of equality of education opportunity. However, there was considerable discrimination in the classroom: African-Caribbean boys received disproportionate amounts of teachers' negative attentions, were more likely to be sent out of class, to be sent to see the head teacher or have privileges withdrawn. (p101). In Wright's earlier case study of a mixed comprehensive school in the Midlands [1988], she noted; "even if teachers did not always intend to be racist, one teacher commented; "I had a Black girl in my class, she did something or another, I said to her, if you're not careful I'll send you back to the chocolate factory...It was only said in good fun, nothing malicious" (pp.199-200). Foster (1990a) criticized the validity of Wright's (1988) conclusions and argued that they were based on little direct evidence, an often uncritical acceptance of and strong reliance on insider accounts, and a tendency to generalize findings on the basis of a small number of cases (in Stevens, 2014, p.158). Foster et al make the following conclusion based on their overall statement in regard to schools and inequality: In short, there is no convincing evidence currently available for any substantial role on the part of schools in generating inequalities in educational outcomes between social classes, genders, or ethnic groups. Studies simply assume that schools play such a role, often on the basis of appeals to reproduction theory and social class constructionism: neither of which can provide the necessary support. (1996, p.174).

Although the chronicling of ethnic underachievement has a long history nationally and internationally, Tomlinson (1989) argues that "pre-1980 research on achievement of minorities should now be treated with caution, as much of it was small-scale and used problematic methodology" (p.21). The dismissal of such research is perhaps correct when seeking to question their design methods, validity and rigour of such reports. However, how does this dismissal absolve the 'planting' of such notions in the reader's mind where 'the deficit other' has been firmly positioned?

Research evidences that the myth of black inferiority is not just a United Kingdom issue but a global phenomenon. Okonofua & Eberhardt (2015) at Stanford University examined the reaction of a sample of secondary and primary school teachers to students' 'race'. They found that the teachers were more likely to view students who they thought were black as troublemakers rather than those they thought were white. "Driven by racial stereotypes can lead teachers to escalate their negative responses to black students over the course of multiple interpersonal e.g. teacher-to-student-encounters' (p.1). In their study, Eberhardt and her colleagues presented teachers with fictional records. These records described two instances of misbehaviour by a student. The teachers were asked about the perception of the severity, how irritated that misbehaviour would make them feel and how the student should be punished. They were asked whether they saw the student as a troublemaker and if they could imagine themselves suspending that pupil in the future. The researchers randomly assigned names to the student records, in some cases suggesting the student was black with names like De-shawn or Darnell and in others, suggesting they were white with names like Greg or Jake. They found that racial stereotypes had little impact on the teachers' views after one infraction. However, the second piece of misbehaviour was seen as 'more troubling' when committed by a black student rather than a white student. The teachers also tended to want to discipline black students more harshly as they were more likely to see misbehaviour as part of a pattern (Gray, 2015 p.2). The authors concluded their findings with a term: 'The Black Escalation Effect', in which "teacher responses may even drive racial differences in student behaviour and differential treatment by teachers, to some extent, may cause repeated misbehaviour by black students" (Okonofua & Eberhardt, 2015, p6).

Does the evidence suggest that teachers deliberately set out to systematically disadvantage black students? The invisibility of whiteness as a social construct remains at the heart of the education system. Indeed, the Rampton Report (1981) made explicit reference to this point: Since a profession of nearly half a million people must, to a great extent; reflect the attitudes of a society at large there must be some teachers who hold explicitly racist views (section 5, p.12). Similarly, Gillborn (2008) argues that "whiteness relates to the ways of knowing and being, the assumptions and actions that characterize white people in this racist society (p.9). Richard Dyer (1988) reminds us that 'white remains the 'unraced' norm against which all difference is measured... cultural investigations of 'race' should not focus on blackness alone, but realize that whiteness is itself a racial concept' (p.46). Philip (2011) and Lowenstein (2009) argue that white teachers do have knowledge about issues of race and there is a tendency to assume that white people do not have any experiences with issues of race or diversity. They argue that "many white teachers have formed some ideas about race, whether they are undeveloped or in some cases misguided" (in Shank 2016, p.32). Similar studies show how well intentioned white teachers demonstrate an inclusive pedagogy and positive interactions with their diverse student populations, however, a lack of self in relation to their privilege remained unexamined (McIntyre, 1997; Pennington, Brock & Ndura, 2012; Henfield & Washington, 2012). Additionally, Pollock (2008) describes teachers who are prepared to engage with issues of race as ones who are conscious and thoughtful about how their everyday actions might perpetuate racial inequality (in Shank, 2016 p.32). In Milner's (2011) study in culturally relevant pedagogy, he observed white teachers who "sustained meaningful relationships with students, confronted matters of race with them and perceived teaching as a communal affair" (p.76).

Culturally responsive (or relevant) teaching has been described by Ladson-Billings (2009) as: "A pedagogy that empowers students intellectually, socially, emotionally, and politically by using cultural referents to impart knowledge, skills and attitudes" (p.20). A common misconception, according to Rajagopal (2011) about culturally responsive pedagogy is that teachers must teach the 'Asian way' or the 'Black way'. People often get intimidated by the words *culturally responsive* because of the incredible number of cultures and mixes of cultures in today's classrooms. "Too often, teachers subscribe to the misguided idea that students of different 'races' need to be taught differently, and they waste an enormous amount of effort in the process" (p.1). Irvine (2009) cites two common examples used by teachers that she observed in mathematics lessons: "Ms Edwards was discouraged because her African American and Latino students were consistently failing her maths tests. After a colleague mentioned her success in using culturally responsive instructional strategies, she decided to experiment. She bought the CD called Multiplication Rap, which promised to teach mathematics based on repetition, rhyme, hand clapping and hip-hop music. She thought the music would appeal to her students' cultural interests. However, in the classroom the students focused on the music itself, paying little attention to the maths objectives, many were unimpressed with the CD and commented on the audio quality and the amateurish lyrics. The 'failure' rate on Ms Edwards' weekly mathematics tests did not change as a result of these interventions" (p.40). Irvine (2010) congratulates the teacher in her efforts to stimulate the students' mathematical thinking. However, she concludes by stating: "Ms Edwards' experience is not uncommon. Many teachers have only a cursory understanding of culturally relevant pedagogy, and their efforts to bridge the cultural gap often fall short" (p.57). Why, then, is music perceived as the starting point for instruction which is exclusively aimed at melanated students? Why is rap music perceived as a 'gateway saviour' for all black students who are perceived as 'failing'? And why do some teachers not consider that their students possess critical thinking and may actually 'see through' the artifice?

Uri Treisman (2001) a professor of mathematics was teaching calculus on his engineering course at Berkeley, and he noticed that the black students were not 'performing' at the same level as the Chinese students in his class. So, he sent out a survey to his teaching colleagues throughout the campus and he asked: "Why do you think that my African American students are performing lower than my Chinese American students"? Treisman (1992) reported: "Let me state what we found in the survey because I believe that these assumptions are responsible for the failure of many university intervention efforts, and because these assumptions are rarely stated explicitly and then, almost never publicly. Four widely-held beliefs about the causes of minority failure: (1) They are less motivated; (2) less well prepared; (3) lack parental support; (4) Income as the dominant variable.

Minority Students' failure could be attributed to all these factors, incidentally and conveniently, over which we had no control" (p.364-365).

Treisman (1992) also pointed out that "of course we had never met any of these families, but we seemed to have clear ideas about them" (ibid), usually negative. Finally, he points out that there may actually be something wrong with the institution. His observations on how different cultural groups studied mathematics revealed very different learning styles for black and Chinese students. The former approached the subject as isolated learners and the latter after classes had ended would reconvene to extend the subject in a social setting.

As a result of these observations, Treisman and his faculty created a re-conceptualized pedagogical programme in which, "the emphasis was on group learning and a community life focused on a shared interest in mathematics; the heart of the program was group learning" (p.368). The ability to continually question, review and reconfigure traditional methodologies into transformative solutions is a very powerful tool, a strategy that cautions the teacher to look outside of firmly held cultural stereotypes. This critical component enabled Treisman (1992) to state: "The results of the program were quite dramatic. Black and Latino participants, typically more than half of all such students enrolled in calculus, substantially outperformed not only their minority peers, but white and Asian classmates as well. Many of the students from these early workshops have gone on to become physicians, scientists, and engineers...and many others have won distinguished graduate fellowships" (p369). The Peer Led Team Learning program (PLTL) was developed in part response to the success of Treisman's research, and these workshops are now in many universities' taught programmes across the United States of America (Preszler, 2009).

As early as 1965, 'The Pygmalion effect' (changes in teachers' expectation produce changes in student achievement) in which, Rosenthal & Jacobson conducted an experiment in a public elementary school, informing teachers that certain children could be expected to be 'growth spurters', based on the students' results on the Harvard IQ Test of Inflected Acquisition. In fact, the test was spurious and those children designated as 'spurters' were chosen randomly. Rosenthal & Jacobson (1968) found that in the first and second grades the effects of teachers' prophesies were dramatic in "relation to total IQ, verbal IQ, and especially reasoning IQ, children of the minority group were more advantaged by receiving favourable treatment in the classroom than the other children" (p 20). The authors concluded their findings by stating: "when teachers expected that certain children would show greater intellectual development, those children *did* show greater intellectual development" (ibid, emphasis added).

The self-fulfilling prophecy evident in the above teacher-effect research, is on one hand very powerful and potentially instructive. However, it has serious implications and weaknesses of design, unethical issues, and stereotypical assumptions made by the teachers for example, in the section under 'Minority Group Status' the authors describe how the students were selected: 'Within this sample of Mexican minority-group children there were variations in how 'Mexican' each child looked. A group of ten teachers with no connection to Oak school or its children rated each photograph on 'how Mexican the child looked'. The definition of how clearly Mexican a child 'really' looked was the average rating of all ten teachers. These ratings were highly reliable' (Rosenthal & Jacobson, 1968 p.17).

The students were selected based on how 'Mexican' they looked and the more pronounced their 'mexican-ness' was used as a strong criterion correlated to their perceived intelligence, and their primary selection was based on this erroneous stereotype. The obviously raises the issue of how ethical can the research be when it is based on deception? Ellison (2015) argues that the expectations that these teachers had for their students were only fruitful when their behaviours were subconsciously driven, suggesting that they might not have been able to so easily alter their own teaching behaviours if they had known the truth about their students from the beginning (p.3). Robert Thorndike (1968), an expert in education and psychological testing, argued that: "Pygmalion is so defective technically that one can only regret that it ever got beyond the eyes of the original investigators!" (p.708). Albert Shanker, founder and future president of the United Federation of Teachers, rebuked the Pygmalion experiment, suggesting that it vilified teachers (in Ellison,2015, p.4). Despite the criticisms and weaknesses in design which would ordinarily invalidate the research results, something positive did happen to those children in the study, namely that they believed in themselves as learners, as thinkers and individuals because of the conducive actions as transmitted and communicated by their classroom teachers.

In a longitudinal study, the importance of the Pygmalion effect and the issue of teacher expectations were analyzed by Boser, Wilhelm & Hana (2014). Their longitudinal research used the National Center for Education Statistics to analyse the achievements of nationally representative annual samples of 10th grade students (aged 15-16) from 2002 to 2012. The study reported the following: 'Secondary teachers had lower expectations for students of colour and students from disadvantaged backgrounds. Non-black teachers of black students had significantly lower expectations than black teachers. These effects are larger for black male students and mathematics teachers. What is clear, however, is that social stereotypes can play a crucial role as teachers build assumptions about their students and their future performance' (pp. 2 & 4). In addition, social-class is seen as an active variable within the Pygmalion effect: 'Working class pupils live up to the lower expectations that (middle-class) teachers hold of them, and in response to these individual or collective notions of institutional failure, they develop disaffected sub-cultural attitudes' (Willis, 1977 in Stevens,2014, p.150).

The early work of Okonofua & Eberhardt (2015) discussed 'The Black Escalating Effect' as a potential outcome of teachers' racial differential treatment; and whether that may drive the misbehaviour of many black students. However, to view black students as a homogenous group negates the power of alternative 'ways of being' in the classroom. Bigford (2013) contends that notions of resilience, identity, and black cultural and social capital are used by African-Caribbean students; this resists the notion of black students being perceived as 'objects of analysis' rather than as 'subjects with agency' (Ackah, 2014). Scholars such as

Sewell (1996), Gillborn (2002), Rhamie (2007) have suggested that a combination of disaffection continued institutional racism and low expectations by teachers mean that black students must develop a particular resilience in order to negotiate schooling successfully (Bigford, 2013 p.13).

Anthropologist John Ogbu's (2004) "oppositional culture theory" argues that black students "resist schooling for fear of 'acting white' and possess a certain culture of speech and behaviours that are in opposition to the dominant culture of schools (p.2). While there are certainly groups of black students who fall within this domain of resistance, other studies have found this analysis problematic. Nieto (2004) raises the issue of groups of students who are "oppositional *and* academically successful as not being presented as a possibility" (p.267). Mac an Ghaill's (1988) study of a sixth form college, with a group of African Caribbean girls, reported on the same theme of being oppositional and academically driven, as proposed by Nieto (2004). Mac an Ghaill (1988) observed: 'The girls responded to perceived racism through *resistance with accommodation* or by adopting a highly instrumental view of teachers and teaching processes in which (culturally biased) knowledge is not valued, but as a means to an end, that of getting qualifications' (p.35, original emphasis).

Wright, Maylor & Becker's (2016) interview based study of 14-19 year old young black students (in Nottingham and Birmingham) who had been excluded from school, found that: "These students' narratives actively resisted their negative school experiences and worked to transform their labelling as 'failures' into a desire to have a positive educational outcome" (p.6). This begs the inevitable question: What happens if I do not possess the psychological tools, maturity or emotional capacity to transform myself, into a strong willed individual capable of navigating an educational system framed within a discourse of *problematic students*?

At the end of the second decade of the twenty first century, it is clear that Black History Month needs a rethink: David Olusoga's (2015) statement that it is time to ditch the heroes (p.1) resonates. It has become perceived as the norm, for some teachers to use role-play which focuses on slavery, brutality, and to make race-based assumptions about a white or black child's relationship to the topic of slavery. To exemplify this contemporary misunderstanding, a school in Rochester, Kent in the United Kingdom has been strongly criticised for asking children to act as slave traders and 'buy' slaves at an auction. Pupils were asked to pretend that they had £100 and were asked to "consider what sort of slave your business will need" (Edwards,2017, p1). Is this an example of the failure of the education system (teachers/school governance) to understand what black history is or rather world history? The notion that black history can be encapsulated in a 'Black History month' is indicative of the narrowness and lack of depth on the subject in the school curriculum. When history is conceptualized within an episodic framework, utilizing isolated disconnected events, it inevitably creates the above scenarios. Instead, teachers need to be encouraged to develop deeper understandings of world history as holistic and connected events. Olusoga (2015) suggests that "in a highly selective 'island story' version of the

British past... slavery was little more than a story of white abolitionists, and the colonial conquest of Africa" (p.2). Keinde Andrews, an associate professor in Sociology at Birmingham City University, specializing in race and racism responded: 'If this is how Black history is taught in schools, then it is better that they do not teach it at all. The levels of insensitivity just tell you how lightly the genocide of African people is viewed in the school system' (in Weale 2017, p.2).

In the United States of America, parents of students at Windsor Hill Elementary School in Los Angeles reported their outrage when children were asked to tackle a mathematics problem based around "how many slaves it would take to fill 75 bags of cotton but only 96 slaves were able to pick cotton for the day" (Judge 2017, p.3). Other current examples, from many classroom practices, include a Californian school which required children to draw a poster for a slave auction. The posters were used as a display in the school's main hall during a teacher-parent conference. Some of the posters showed smiling, brightly coloured paintings of slaves as runaways; Karriem (2017) argued "educating young students on the harsh realities of slavery was not the problem however, the medium is grossly insensitive and negligent" (in Edwards. B, 2017, p.6). A New Jersey school held a 'mock' slave auction in which a black 5th Grader was 'sold' by the white children in the class (Roundtree, 2017). In a recent study Shank (2016) challenges the notion that all white teachers should be viewed as one homogenous group who think and teach in an undifferentiated manner. In her work she observed that the White teachers in the four schools she visited: '... demonstrated a strong level of racial awareness as well as culturally responsive and multicultural teaching practices. This included a pedagogy that ensured equity for students, and multicultural content integration; they also acknowledged the socio-emotional needs of the students in their classrooms' (p. ii).

Earlier examples which highlighted the lack of cultural understanding in many classrooms clearly need to be addressed however, the literature evidences that there are many educators with a developing understanding of the needs of their diverse students in their classrooms. Much work is still required in order that comprehensive narratives of cultural understandings and history are being taught. As a consequence, the prevailing invisibility of those comprehensive models through the absence of an empowerment curriculum content means that if everything that I, (as a black child) am taught has zero relevance to my identity, what do I have to model from and aspire to? Has the black child become an object of analysis within a narrowed definition of intelligence, creativity and possibility and labelled as a failure in performance league tables terms? (Charles, 2017, p.2). In addition, not only is the black student not being empowered, *all students* are potentially experiencing similarly distorted versions of culture, history and the creation and development of worldwide civilizations.

The importance of social community cohesion is one of the major goals of schooling because education is the most revolutionary process in any society; if inclusive, it automatically transforms vulnerable groups into empowered individuals (Johnson 2015; Freire 1976). The researcher's findings (2004, 2010, 2016, 2019) have implications for how young learners view and internalize knowledge construction and identify themselves as empowered learners. The researcher supports Irvine's (1988) assertion that: 'A lack of black teachers promotes the idea that teaching is a white profession and serves as a disincentive for black students to select the teaching profession for themselves' (p.509). A deeper understanding of who actually controls and conducts the process of educating our students is often seen as an irrelevant or trivial analysis. However, if a school is a function of community, a function of society and a function of culture, should that school not reflect the diversity and inclusiveness of society? (Johnson 2015; Apple 2001; Bonilla-Silva 2010; Hall,2007; Ladson-Billings 2005). Culture is often misunderstood as simply the observance of rituals, and celebrations whilst they are important, they are often used superficially as a panacea for all students' needs and identities.

Culture is the invisible meaning in which all human functioning occurs, it is important to note that nothing happens outside of culture. Culture is to the human what water is to a fish. It is our total environment and like the fish out of water, some students can be out of their culture and thereby act inappropriately or fail to thrive' (Nobles 2010, p1). Culture is also about solving problems. Ultimately, that is why people evolve a culture, so when a culture no longer solves the problems of a particular group or meets the needs of those groups, then it must be transformed (Wilson,1993; Jones 1990). The different cultures that are present in every classroom (teachers and students), have been viewed by Bourdieu (1986/2011) namely, that some cultures are valued more than others. Bourdieu proposed the term "cultural capital to describe the beliefs, knowledge, and sense of self that is closely linked to a person and has value in the marketplace of society" (p.85).

Lana Guinier (2004) is hugely relevant here because of her work on the 'ideal learner' (white, male and middle class) which provides a relevant framework for understanding the racialized experiences within British school life. Her term, 'racial literacy', has three components: first, 'racial literacy' involves flexibly approaching problems, being experimental, reflective and active towards solutions; second, racial literacy centres the significance of 'race' and its relationship to institutional power. Finally, keeping sight of individuals' agency against power but recognizing that oppressive structures maintain and delimit that agency within an existing system' (p.100). Equally important is 'History is not the mere calling of past events or the recapitulation of dates and times, it is our total orientation towards and within the world. The past lives in your brain, in your behaviour, the way you see life and the way you see yourself' (Wilson 1993 p.28).

It is the reclamation of factual history (Van Sertima 2005) viewed not through a myopic lens, which propagates historical distortions, but a history that seeks to "rescue, reclaim and restore African world history" (Levi, 2012, p.180). This factual history will evidence that a melanated presence in the United Kingdom is measured in millennia, not decades as Reid (2014) argues, and, it is within this paradigm of holistic understanding that the author's pedagogical programme of reframed curriculum units has been conceptualized.

Chapter 3: Afrocentricity and Africana Phenomenology: A Theoretical Base

Afrocentricity is informed by an African episteme that is, by ways of knowing and conceptions of knowledge based on African worldview and the cultural concepts that express that worldview. (King & Swartz, 2018, p.26). King & Swartz (2018) posit that this theory sits within the academic discipline of Africology and provides many theories in many fields and disciplines (Asante, 2008; Bethel, 2003; Cokely, 2003; Dove, 1998; Mazama, 2003). Specifically, Africology 'Is the central element of Africological research and is interlaced with the ongoing transdisciplinarity of Africology [9](African Diaspora Studies, African Studies, Africana Studies, African American Studies, Black Studies, Pan African Studies etc. Afrocentricity is an intellectual, philosophical and theoretical perspective deriving its name from the centrality of African people and phenomena in the interpretation of data (Flemming, 2017, p.319).

As an intellectual theory, Afrocentricity is the study of the ideas and events from the standpoints of Africans as the key players rather than victims. This theory becomes, by virtue of an authentic relationship to the centrality of our own reality, a fundamentally empirical project...it is Africa asserting itself intellectually and psychologically (Asante, 1991, p.172). King & Swartz (2018) trace this legacy to the late nineteenth and early decades of the twentieth century. Scholars in the Black intellectual tradition: "Conducted research and wrote about ideas and practices that fostered self-determination, community uplift, and indigenous accounts of Black history" (p.27). (Dubois, 1899, 1903, 1920, 1935/1972; Bond, 1934, 1935; Cooper, 1892/1969; Miller, 1908; Wells, 1892; Woodson, 1919a, 1919b, 1933/2010). This intellectual tradition has cultural continuity with other Diasporan scholars over two centuries. (Crummel, 1898; Fanon, 1963, 1965; Fontaine, 1940; Jones, 1958; Padmore, 1931, 1969, 1971; John, 1971, 1976; Garnet, 1843/1972; Grant et al, 2016; Hilliard, 1978, 2003; King, 2004, 2015; Mills, 1997; Walker, 1829/1965; Wynter, 2006). Scholars from the last thirty years of the twentieth century shaped the nomenclature of their predecessors into the modern term Afrocentricity and extended the rich scholarship that had gone before. It is, correctly conceptualized as a location in which African people speak for, define, and name themselves: (Alkebulan, 2007; Asante,1988, 1998, 2011; Bankole, 1995; Karenga, 2003, 2006a; Kershaw, 1992, 2003; Mazama, 2003b).

One of the leading contemporary theorists, professor Molefi Kete Asante (2003) states: "Afrocentricity creates inter alia, a critique of social history" (p.61). This necessary understanding of 'among other things' in defining inter alia is the multiple perspectives that exist in the cultural production of knowledge with its interpretive framework understood as both a liberating and freeing event.

---

[9] "The *black world* is perceived as patterns within a quinti-lateral relationship between Africa, the trilateral *black world* model (Turner, 2016, p.170). African Caribbean, the African Americas, African American and African European. Moreover, all segments of the black world population live under social conditions directly related to the international political economy of advanced industrial capitalism. I (Charles), have expanded James Turner's (1984) original model.

These definitions are crucial in understanding the theoretical underpinnings of Afrocentricity. The importance of this not only aids clarification, but it dispels the common held errors alongside crude misunderstandings of this paradigm. For example, sociologist Patricia Hill Collins (1991) states Afrocentricity is the participation in "a core African value system coupled with the experience of oppression" (p.206). However, Mazama (2003) argues: "Afrocentricity stresses the importance of cultivating a consciousness of victory as opposed to dwelling on oppression" (p.6).In similar confusion, author and political scientist Russell Adams (1993) contends "the purest form of Afrocentrism places Africa at its center as the source of the world's people and its most fundamental ideas and inventions" (p.34). This interpretation is somewhat problematic as it suggests the negation and entitlement of other cultural groups' practices and celebrations. Indeed, Asante (1988) makes it quite clear: "All people have a perspective which stems from their centers...while Eurocentrism imposes itself as universal; Afrocentrism demonstrates that it is only one way to view the world (pp.87-9). Indeed Asante (2003) adds further clarification for the uninitiated: 'I have always believed that Eurocentricity was possible as a normal expression of culture but could be abnormal if it imposed its cultural particularity as universal while denying and degrading other cultural political or economic views (p.61).

Professor Molefi Kete Asante (1980; 1987; 1990), is recognized as one of the leading Afrocentric scholars in the field of Africology and is the pioneer of the first PhD in this discipline at Temple University. Throughout his career, he has consciously and explicitly explained that this paradigm, is not conceptualized as universal, hegemonic or supreme: "It secures its place alongside other centric pluralisms without hierarchy and without seeking hegemony" (Asante,1990, p.12). It is important that researchers clearly define, examine and express the fundamental differences between a paradigm that takes up all the 'space' for example, as an imposition on everybody else as the only way to look at the world; and this imposition is an ethnocentric idea that values the European experience above all other experiences. Within these parameters, Asante's (1988) quote above may be problematic in his use of the word Afrocentrism as opposed to Afrocentricty, historian Maulana Karenga (2003) (creator of Kwanzaa and its seven principles-Nguzo Saba), articulates the important distinctions between the two terms: 'I prefer and use Afrocentricity for several reasons: to stress its intellectual value as distinct from its ideological use; to clearly distinguish it from Eurocentricism which is an ideology of domination and exclusion. For Afrocentricity must never be conceived or employed as a reaction to or an African version of Eurocentricism with its racist and structured denial and deformation of the history and humanity of peoples of colour (pp. 76-77).

Karenga (2003) is keen to separate ideology from an intellectual domain, which he views as being connected and tied to a legacy of domination and exclusion however, ideology as tied to ideas, (Asante, 2017) can and should be viewed, as positive and progressive. All societies can be said to be ruled by ideas and without them, their cultural members will not know how to form a connection between one Diaspora and another Diaspora, i.e. Jamaica, Haiti, USA, Brazil, Britain, in fact all over the world to sustain and promulgate an intellectual idea. Within this episteme, it is positive because Ideology involves a prophetic vision of a thought as well as action orientation of a moral commitment to serve. Thus, ideology combines an interpretation of the social world with a moral commitment to change it (Alkalimat & McWorter, 1969, p.28).

Fundamentally, this aspect requires additional clarification within an academic context, which delineates Afrocentricity as a paradigm (Maat & Carroll, 2012; Mazama, 2012; Levi, 2012; Tillotson, 2011; Yehudah, 2015). For Masterman (1970): "Paradigms are a puzzle-solving device...paradigm is a way of seeing" (p.59). While Bloor (1976) defines a paradigm: "as an exemplary piece of scientific work which creates a research tradition within some specialized area of scientific enquiry" (p.57). Thomas Kuhn's (1962) book: *Structure of Scientific Revolutions* (SSR) refers to a paradigm as a dominant mode of thinking shared by a scientific community (1962;1970; 2012); this mode of thinking is termed 'normal science' however, Kuhn's ideas challenged the taken for granted assumptions held by the practitioners of 'normal science' and proposed:"This in turn led to the idea that a new theory was not chosen to replace an old one because it was true but more because of a *change in worldview* (2012, p. x, original emphasis).

Kuhn questioned the idea of scientific neutrality and universality as untenable and, in doing so, alerted social scientists, researchers and philosophers to probe their modes of enquiry and make explicit these assumptions in disciplinary recognition. Indeed, he argued: 'That true breakthroughs arise in totally different ways; when the discovery of anomalies leads scientists to question the paradigm and this in turn, leads to a scientific revolution, that is termed paradigmatic shift' (Kuhn, ibid, p. xxiii).

Within these parameters, Afrocentricity as a paradigmatic shift asks different sorts of questions that other paradigms cannot answer as they are operating from their own distinct methodological lens. For example, '*Why is this interpretation ignoring the locations where this phenomena, can be found/traced/used*? i.e. *The book of Khun- Anup*, is the oldest treatise on social justice (Lichtheim, 1975) and *The Book of Ptahhotep* which offers a discourse on leadership as a moral vocation (Lichtheim, 1975; Simpson, 1973). The solution, for Asante (2018) is the acceptance of African people who are centred in their own historical narratives. 'Therefore, Afrocentricity is a paradigm in which African people must view themselves in an historical context as centred within the framework of their own realities and experiences- this is what Afrocentricity is. It is a simple proposition that is not against anybody. It is an understanding of *all* people and it does not deny anybody of anything' (Speech given at Temple University on PhD programme).

This important shift in thinking rests on two central aspects to a paradigm as defined by Kuhn: the cognitive and structural components but, for Mazama (2003), Hassan (2013) and Masterman (1970) to focus on these two features in isolation is to limit the effectiveness of the paradigm being platformed. Researchers and social scientists, who focus on 'thinking', and 'being' exclusively, neglect the necessary components of 'feeling' and 'doing'. Put simply, the affective, conative and cognitive aspects of the Afrocentric paradigm. Masterman (1970) suggests:"there is a tendency to depend on the metaphysical and cognitive so much that they have forgotten to allow for the material and practical that are a large part of normal science (p.71). There is a tendency for some researchers in producing research methodology to enter into discursive spaces only and not to exit into praxis. Cultural theorist and linguist, Ama Mazama (2003), contends that Kuhn's definition of a paradigm is important in terms of the cognitive, affective and structural components i.e. the community of scholars who practice the cognitive dimension of the paradigm; however, it is limited in one crucial regard: 'Namely a *functional aspect*...from an Afrocentric perspective, where knowledge can never be produced, for the sake of it, but always for the sake of our liberation, *a paradigm must activate our consciousness* to be of any use to us (p.8, original emphasis).

Psychologist, William Curtis Banks (1992), called this vital paradigmatic component: teleology, in which, "the absence of this dimension deprives the framework of an essential source of justification (p.266). More pointedly: 'This teleological assumption impacts an Africana Studies research methodology in that it suggests that there is an intended goal for research, scholarship and intellectual projects that we produce. This must be seen in distinction to 'knowledge for knowledge sake', which is so common within the western intellectual tradition (Carroll, 2008, p.16).

The author's pedagogical Reframed Units of Change (RUoCs) comprise the core epistemic foundation for this book and have been conceptualized and written to embrace the rigour and requirement within the triangulated aspects of this paradigm. It is, as King and Swartz (2018) assert, a conscious attempt to "return what you learn to the people" in the tradition of the freedom schools pedagogy (Clark, 1964; Cobb, 2011; Coard, 1971; Humphry & John, 1971), and the emancipation work of Paulo Freire (1970). McNiff & Whitehead (2000) suggest that it is time to move beyond a vision of linear progress, which goes from **A---B---C** and therefore, must be rooted in an ontology, of *being*: dynamic, free-flowing and unique like a crystallized snowflake with its intricate structures of branching and symmetry [see Figure 7 below].

 **Figure 7: Branching and symmetry of thinking**

This, then moves, towards a generative transformational process, which develops in an iterative way and engages with an ontology of *becoming* (p.8). The final stage, or rather essential element in methodology should have "reconciliation among humans in relation to their environment" i.e. *belonging* (ibid).

The canon of Black intellectual scholars as cited earlier, created many ideas and modes of thought that systematically built upon this tradition over several centuries. This incrementalized cultural process has now been projected into the present to shape

Afrocentric theoretical concepts (see Figure 8 below). These concepts have a foundational African episteme for example: the African cultural concept of *knowing as a communal experience in which everyone has something to contribute* (Akbar, 1984; Fu-Kiau, 2001; Nkulu-N'Senga, 2005), has an origin in the *Book of Khun-Anup* (moral justice) and the *Book of Ptahhotep* (moral leadership) Lichtheim 1975; Simpson, 1973.

Collective Consciousness: This epistemology refers to the "retention of the ancestral sensibilities within and across generations (Nobles, 2005, p.199). This way of knowing conveys the historic continuity of African essence, energy, and excellence: sustained through relationships within the collective African family and make awareness, knowledge , and meaning possible and elicits value for the human collective.

Centrality/Location: Placing Africa and African people and experiences at the centre of the phenomena means that African knowledge and *being* are a location or standing place from which the past and previous can be viewed and understood.

Subjects with Agency: African people are subjects when and where they are present. They have will and capacity to act in and on the world-not only as individuals but also as members of their cultural group.

Reclamation of Cultural Heritage: The conscious recovery of African history, culture, and identity that is grounded in knowledge of African cosmology, ontology, epistemology, and axiology; and presented with a culturally authentic lexicon is a model for reclaiming the heritage of diverse cultures.

Anteriority of Classical African Civilizations: Ancient Kemet and prior African civilizations developed and exhibited the earliest demonstrations of excellence in foundational disciplines such as philosophy, mathematics, science, medicine, the arts and architecture (King & Swartz, 2018, p.28)

Figure 8: Afrocentric concepts

The theoretical concept of: '*Subjects with Agency'* is particularly important as it reaffirms the many historical endeavours such as the building of the pyramids in Kemet, and the Songhai, Mali & Ghana Empires, to name just a few, in which, "African people had the will and capacity to develop democratic systems of governance (King & Swartz, 2018, p.30). This theoretical concept rejects the axiological, research domain of viewing black participants as 'objects of measurement' (Ackah, 2014; Nichols, 1986), in which black individuals are interviewed notionally for their perspectives on areas of 'disadvantage'. This, is then, usually followed up with an array of statistical quantification including graphs and charts only for the participants never to hear from the researcher or the research again. "We seem to be overwhelmed with academic social science on race...doing little more than quantify the obvious" (Humphry & John, 1972, p.10).

Psychologist Robert Williams (2008) describes how this phenomenon called; 'objects of measurement' first recorded in 1968: '...Calling a halt, to the abuse of Black communities by white researchers who use data taken from such communities to advance themselves professionally and economically while those studied continue to exist as a powerless people' (ABPsi- press release in September 1968, p.4)
Richards (1989) concludes by stating as researchers within the discipline of
 'Afrocentricity we must not be afraid to create new concepts, theories and methodologies connected to *being, feeling, seeing and knowing* . It is perhaps more beneficial to articulate "I think, therefore WE are, as a vision of the future in connection to our research projects.' [p.32]

Mazama (2003) reminds us that affective and conative domains are central to Afrocentricity. Dixon (1976) summarizes the epistemological assumption of the Euro-American worldview: 'I step back from phenomena, I reflect; I measure; I think; I know; and therefore I am and I feel. While the Afrikan epistemological assumption states I feel phenomena; therefore, I think; I know. The centrality of 'empty perceptual space' is found within the Euro-American assumption which 'steps back', while the Afrikan does not, thus negating the existence of 'empty perceptual space' (in Carroll, 2008, p.11).

The question of epistemology as it relates to worldview differences is critical in regard, to the role of objectivity within social science research. Valentine (2016) traces the influential work of Ayn Rand (born Alisa Zinovyevna Rosenbaum), philosopher, founder of *Objectivism* and the author of the book *Atlas shrugged*. Rand & Branden (1962) promulgated "the theory of individualism as a central component of the Objectivist Philosophy (p.13); underscored with the view that the proper purpose in one's life is to pursue "one's happiness through rational self interest. He must exist for his own sake and his own happiness is the highest moral purpose of his life" (p.35). Rand continued in her philosophical positioning at a lecture on 'The *Objectivist Ethics*' at the Massachusetts Institute of Technology in 1962, in which she addressed an audience of future scientists: 'I believe that many of you were attracted to the field of social sciences precisely by reason of that dichotomy: in order to escape from the hysterical mystic-subjectivist emotionalist shambles to which philosophers have reduced the field in order to find a clean, intelligible, rational *objective* realm of activity' (p.41, original emphasis).

Rand (1962) sharply delineates the episteme: 'Object-Measure-Cognition' worldview as argued by philosopher Vernon Dixon (1976). She rejects the Afrikan affective personalizing worldview of the phenomenal world as 'hysterical, mystic-subjectivist emotionalist shambles'. Here, the separation of the mind and body (dualism), and the dichotomous logic influences of Plato, Hegel, Descartes and Kant and Locke are observable as Rand's 'clean, intelligible, rational objective realm is utilized, in order to justify the following statement on indigenous nations and First World People (FWP): 'The Native American did not have any rights to the land and there was no reason for anyone to grant them rights. Any white person who brought the element of civilization had the right to take over this continent' (in Mayhew, 2005, pp. 102 &104).

In a similar vein, Ayn Rand (1999) describes FWP: 'A South American aborigine who is devoured by piranha in a jungle stream- an African who is bitten by the tsetse fly-an Arab whose teeth are green with decay in his mouth-these do live with their 'natural environment' but are scarcely able to appreciate its beauty' (p.166). Rand (1999) echoes the sentiments of her philosophical predecessors who viewed the 'Othering' of melanated human beings as extensions of the flora and fauna of the 'New World', which is to be essentially controlled and subdued by a more 'clean, intelligible, rational and objective realm'. Note, the confluence of Rand, Montesquieu (1800), and Hegel's (1840/1956) statements: "Africa proper is the gold-land compressed" (p.91). 'They are savages and barbarians...they [negroes], are without industry or arts...they have gold in abundance which they receive immediately from nature"..."The Negroes prefer a glass necklace to the gold which polite nations so highly value" (Montesquieu,1800, *Spirit of Laws vol 1*, p.20 & p.282).

This axiomatic framing captures the essence of how 'objects' are to be sought after, and ultimately controlled within a particular value system that sees nature as an entity to be commodified and dominated. This presumption was reflected in Francis Bacon's (1620) thesis that nature was a thing to be used for human benefit (Carruthers,1999, pp 42-45): "Let the human race recover that right over nature which belongs to it by divine bequest" (p.223). Therefore, these scholars negate the possibility of, and dare to ask: How can indigenous people have a subjective understanding of their own environment, land and culture? Indeed, the founder of the Ayn Rand Institute, philosopher Leonard Peikoff (2012) claims that if you "were to study savages in the jungle you would find that they are mentally undeveloped and thus have no method and no discovery of any control over their minds" (in Wikipedia, 2018 p. 2). If, we as researchers; are claiming to be non- biased, non-racist and non-sexist then this should be clearly stated rather than making bold claims of neutrality, impartiality and objectivity. To claim this axis is a somewhat, untenable position to claim to possess as all people, regardless of status, role and economic standing, are impacted by culture; that neither a-political' nor a-cultural actually exist (Akoto & Akoto, 1999; Hilliard, 2003). According to sociologist, Eric Grollman (2016); "like the myths of meritocracy and color-blindness, objectivity sounds good in theory but it is impossible in practice" (p.1).

Within an Afrocentric theoretical paradigm, Carroll (2008) raises the question of epistemology in relation to perspective and the researcher's worldview; as being intimately tied to the importance of etymology. The term 'object' is at the root of 'objectivity' therefore, closer analysis reveals: 'Etymologically, the root of the term 'object'— 'ject' comes from the

Middle French 'jeter' - to throw. Therefore, at the heart of objectivity is the need to throw space or distance between yourself and what you are studying. This separation is consistent with the need for 'empty perceptual space' as discussed by Dixon (1976). The question of 'objectivity'; should be understood as rooted in the European proclivity for *separation and distinction*. The question of 'objectivity' is probably the most explicit imposition of this culturally-specific epistemological assumption of modern day research process (p.12).

Indeed, sociologist Patricia Leavy (2017), concurs: "Those working from critical worldviews; may find objectivity, not only impossible, but also undesirable as they actively seek to advance social or political agenda" (p.39). It is within this paradigm, that this book is currently positioned; as a way of enlarging an Africana episteme and moving away from a dominant hegemonic view of *being, feeling, seeing* and *knowing*. Therefore, one may probe the inevitable question: Does this create a sense of disequilibrium for the researcher?. Kuhn (2012) reminds us that any paradigmatic shift in the social sciences is a revolutionary act therefore, according to psychologist and cultural theorist Linda Myers (1993), the answer to the question is 'no', if the researcher adopts and understands the term 'diunital'. This concept refers to "something apart and united at the same time" (Dixon, 1971, p.27). Dixon's (1976) earlier contention of Object-Measure- Cognition' is replaced with Affect-Symbolic- Imagery Cognition' (in Carroll, 2088, p11): 'Affect personalizes the phenomenal world. It is one factor in the affect mode of knowing. Affect however, is not intuition, for the latter term means direct knowledge or immediate knowledge (instinctive knowledge) without resource to reference from reason or reason about evidence. Affect does interact with evidence, evidence in the form of symbolic imagery' (Carroll, ibid).

Clarifying the concept of symbolic imagery, Dixon states it is the use of phenomena (words, gestures, tones, rhythms, objects etc) to convey meaning (ibid). This complementary synthesis is conducive to diunital logic: "A person becomes oriented towards a harmonious oneness between the observer and the observed, in which, there is an absence of empty perceptual space among phenomena (ibid). This axiological position recognizes the full humanity of the participants as it seeks an accordant quest for wholeness. Not only through a new historiography of location (Asante 2007), but equally, through intellectual work that: "allows the community to enter; as well as the contention that their entrance should be literally the *conceptual foundation* for understanding and applying knowledge that purports to be about them" (Myers, 2012, p.57 original emphasis). Historian, sociologist and activist, DuBois (1903), exemplifies the very idea that he articulates in the forethought to *The Souls of Black Folk*: "And finally, need I add that I who speak here am bone of the bone and flesh of the flesh of them that live within the veil? (p.209). Myers (2012) argues: "Du Bois articulates that he *is;* who he is studying. The scholar is both participant *and* observer and for historical subjects, both the descendant *and* the observer (p.63). In Kemetic tradition, the *Sesh*, was more than a scribe, the sesh was both researcher and documenter of knowledge (Obenga, 2004).

Therefore, within an Africana episteme, here is the first recorded method of investigation of a given problem-using the correct method using accurate reckoning. This is the ancient and historical blueprint which all social scientists begin their research study with:

" tep: The stage of stating the Given Problem

mi djed en. Ek: This is the stage of defining all of the parts and facets of the problem. The expression *mi djed* means 'according to that which is said', that is the process of reasoning to be addressed to a precisely formulated problem.

peter or pety: The stage of analysis and questioning with the function of eliciting a logical predicate. At this stage then, the student is directly required to ponder and analyze (*ptr-peter*) the problem under examination.

iret mi kheper: The stage of establishing a procedure, or process of showing truth by reasoning and computation.

rekhet.ef pw; The arrival at a clear and certain solution

seshemet, seshmet: Examination of the Proof and this is the review of the whole body of evidence or premises and rules that determine the validity of a solution. Such an examination of a logical proof always leads to a further conceptual generalization. Thus, the ancient Kemites had the technique of forming concepts inductively.

gemi.ek nefer: This is the concluding stage. To find *gemi* is to obtain intellectual effort and bring oneself to a mental awareness of what is correct, precise, perfect (*nefer*). To arrive at a logical conclusion and find that the conclusion withstands critical scrutiny is an achievement in the art of deduction. The rigor of the entire process is evident in the method and the result is objectively known in all truth.
(Obenga, 2004, pp. 41-42; ACE (African Creation Energy), 2010, pp.148-149.

There are two main reasons for this example to prime this chapter; firstly, to situate the authors' epistemological grounding with First World Peoples (FWP), *how do I know what I know?* Secondly, to demonstrate and locate the roots of the original conceptualization of the tradition known as methodology in contemporary society. This ancient Kemetic[10] tradition *rekhet* (knowledge-science and the inquiry into the nature of things), *khet*, is thousands of years old and is evidenced with an African philosophical investigation of causes and laws underlying reality (Obenga, 2015; Diop, 1981,1989; Finch,1990; Browder,1992; Clarke, 1993; Karenga; 2006b; Barashango,1989,1991; Nobles, 2006, 2015; Mazama, 2003; Asante, 2002). In continuation, etymologically, the word 'philosophy' is not of Greek origin (Asante, 2009, Obenga 2004, Finch, 1996). It comes into English and other European languages from Greek but this is not the place of its genesis:

> Philo, which means cherished or loved in the passive; loving and benevolent in the active, and is really less commonly used. Philo, is also used as a substantive to mean friend, brother, or lover. The term philo or philos has no indo-European origin. The second part of the compound is 'sophos' which means literally 'who has

---

[10] Kemet, Greece, China, Axum (Ethiopia), and India may be the most significant civilisations of antiquity. However, in the western world, Egypt and Greece have played dominant roles in the construction of science, philosophy and social ethics. (in Asante & Mazama, 2002, p.1)

knowledge of a technique' or 'one who knows'. Therefore, we can say 'philosophia' is the love of wisdom (Asante, 2011, p.3).

The origin of 'sophia' is clearly in the African language, Mdu Ntr, the language of ancient Egypt, where the word 'Seba' meaning 'the wise' appears first in 2052 BC in the tomb of Anef I, long before the existence of Greece or Greek. The word became 'Sebo' in Coptic and 'Sophia' in Greek. As to the philosopher, the lover of wisdom, that is precisely what is meant by' Seba', the Wise, in ancient tomb writings of the Egyptians (Asante, 2014, p.2).

The Greek word 'sophos' is derived from the Egyptian *seba, sbo sabe*. It is quite exact from the point of view of the history of philosophy to say that philosophy is of African origin; since Egypt is an African country and the first definition of 'the sage, the philosopher' in the history of mankind is to be found in Africa, specifically Egypt (Obenga, 1992, p.60).

The historical origin and antecedence of philosophy in ancient Egyptian civilization has been affirmed as an African civilization (Morakinyo, 2016; Obenga,1992; Diop,1974). How can philosophy be of Greek essence or origin if the word philosophy itself is not a Greek word? (Obenga, 1992, p.54). It is therefore, critical, as Monges (1997) urges that we put the 'head back on Africa' to restore the dislocations and disorientations that colonialism has instituted. Egypt has been 'taken out' of Africa and the Africans out of Egypt. " Egypt was removed from the African continent and placed in the mysterious 'Middle East', a term that was invented by Europeans at the beginning of the 20th century" (Lewis, 1998, p.3). In consequence, Levi (2012) argues that this "geographical and paradigmatic shift was simultaneously accomplished" (p.189). Historian Anthony Browder (1992) also carefully traces the indigenous name and shows how this semantic erosion created the word 'Egypt':

"**Heku Ptah** (the spirit on the hill), then became **Aegupotus**, then **Aegopt** and finally **Egyp**t" (p.51). The UNESCO (1974) symposium on *The Peopling of Africa and the Deciphering of the Meriotic Script* in Cairo, was attended by 'Egyptologists' from all over the world; professors Obenga & Diop (1974) correctly redefined Egypt as Kemet (Kmt). Levi (2012) states: "we are also clear that the ancient people of the Nile valley also defined themselves as Kemtiou - literally 'The Black People' (p.183). Dr Chancellor Williams (1987) reminds us of the importance of using the earliest African name to describe the land:

Before that the country was called Chem (Khem) or Chemi (Khemi)- another name indicating its black inhabitants, and not the colour of the soil, as some writers have needlessly strained themselves in asserting (p.65).

In Plato's book: '*Laws*' written in 360BCE he discusses the importance of education in Kemet (Egypt) and how their teachings and systems made human beings more human. In direct contrast to the 'ignorance' in Greece, he states: "it seemed to me to be the condition of guzzling swine rather than of human beings, and I am ashamed, not only of myself, but of all the Greek world" (p.819e). 'They are like pigs' Obenga (2016) observes and that Greece from its own Greek sources did not have a 'sophia' philosophy of education or methodology it simply did not exist. According to philosopher Lewis Gordon (2007), the linguistic and etymological evidence "challenges an organizing myth in the study of Western intellectual history and the history of philosophy that philosophy is of Greek origin (p.2). This idea of the Greek origin of philosophy is a myth. Plato's writing is very clear that this episteme is not in place in Greece; if you do not have the linguistic foundations- the words, how can you apply it in your institutions and structures? Therefore, "philosophy begins first with the black skinned people of the Nile valley around 2800 BC, that is 2200 years before the appearance of Thales of Miletus, considered the first Western philosopher (Asante, 2004, p.5). In George G.M James' (1954, 2013) seminal text: *Stolen Legacy* he raises several important facts, one of which state:

> The Athenians sentenced Socrates to death (Zeller's 1886/1931 History of
> Philosophy, p.112) and subsequently caused Plato and Aristotle to flee for their lives
> from Athens, because philosophy was
> something foreign and unknown to them (p.16).

Similarly, Kush (2012) observes that this doctrine, as philosophy, "came from an outside and foreign source and contained strange ideas with which they were unacquainted and this prejudice led to the policy of persecution" (p.222). James (1954) also reminds us that our disorientations in relation to the ancient world, needs constant reorientation and restoration as some assumptions distort the natural geographical trajectory and movement of ideas. For example, he states:

> Egyptian philosophy first spread to Ionia [ancient region of Anatolia-present day
> Turkey], thence to Italy and thence to Athens. And it must be remembered that at
> this remote period of Greek history, i.e. Thales to Aristotle 640 BC-322 BC, the
> Ionians were not Greek citizens but first Egyptian subjects and later Persian subjects
> (p.16);   Zeller, 1886/1931; Turner, 1903; Roger, 1908; Alexander, 1907; Sandford,
> 1938.

Indeed, philosopher and literary theorist Philip Wheelwright (1988) notes; "One of the great significant steps in the development of human thought took place at the Ionian city of Miletus in the sixth century B.C (p.40). Note, this date is almost two thousand years after the tomb of Anef I in which Seba, the wise first appeared. Thales of Miletus the Ionian, known by Western traditions as the 'Father of Philosophy', and Diogenes Laertius a third century historian, who observed: "He was one of the Seven Sages, and he was the first to receive the name in the archonship of Damasias at Athens" (p.23). Professor Theophile Obenga (2015), philosopher, historian and linguist evidences that the Greeks themselves recorded this information and that Thales had no association whatsoever with Babylonia in Mesopotamia (the land between the Tigris and Euphrates Rivers). Diogenes Laertius confirms that Thales "having learnt geometry from the Egyptians, went to Egypt and spent some time with the priests there" (pp. 27 & 29)."Thales's pursuit of instruction saw him go by sea (*pleo*, to sail) to Egypt, where he spent time with (*sun-diatribo*) the Egyptian priests (*tois hiereusi*, dative case) Obenga (2015) p.166.

In addition, Finch (1996) asserts that the number of Greeks who lived and learned in Egypt reads like a 'Who's Who' of Greek Philosophy': Solon, Thales, Pythagoras, Eudoxus, Anaximander, Anaxagoras, Democritus, Plato, Archimedes, Hipparchus, Ptolemy, Herophilus, Galen and others too numerous to mention who pursed their higher studies in the Nile valley. As scholars and researchers in the pursuit of the profound yet simple philosophical quest: '*what is it*? From antiquity to present, this has remained constant and is the driver of investigative questions, projects and areas of enquiry, as this signals the need to affirm and reaffirm the epistemological, axiological and ontological location of the researcher in the quest for wholeness. Put simply, one's cultural knowledge, values and nature of being move and shape the project in distinctive ways. As Finch (1996) delineates the numerous Greek scholars that are enshrined in our psyches, their African teachers as the progenitors of philosophy; have been thoroughly omitted, distorted and simply airbrushed out of history. The Greek scholars taught within schools and universities are very important, and their excellence as talented, creative and inventive individuals must continue as celebrations alongside their intellectual contributions. No-one would deny their genius as Asa Hilliard (2002) observes: "brilliant and wise people always seek the most developed tradition and the most developed science" (p.61). Therefore, knowledge always builds upon knowledge and does not exist in a vacuum. How familiar are the names: Ptahotep (2414 BC), Kagemni (2300 BC), Duauf (1400 BC), Amenhotep (1500 BC), Amenemope (1300 BC), Imhotep (2700 BC), Amenemhat (1991 BC), Merikare (1990 BC), Sehotepibre (1991), Khunanup (2040 BC), and Akenaton (1400 BC) in our constructs of knowledge and in our search for the foundational philosophical pursuit of *'what is it'?'*. This quest for wholeness is a call for a new historiography of location (Asante, 2009; Kuhn,1979; Carruthers 1999;). "This kind of historiography is the overcoming of ethnocentric and presentist biases, that is, the projection of the present into the past "(Hoyningen-Huene,1992, p.488)

Is this episteme - ways of knowing, essentialism in its purest form? What are the limitations in Afrocentric theory? To speak of an African way of knowing in research activities and to engage in an intellectual discourse raises the issue of a critique or as Mazama (2002), Karenga (2003) and Asante (2018) suggest, an attack; on being essentialist or essentializing the black experience. Philosopher, Kwame Appiah wrote in his (2010) paper: *Europe Upside Down: Fallacies of the New Afrocentrism*; "That there is unanimism, the view that there is an African culture to which to appeal is surely preposterous (p.50). In a similar vein, historian Clarence Walker (2001) in his book: *Can't go home: An argument about Afrocentrism* posits: "Afrocentrism is a mythology that is racist, reactionary, and essentially therapeutic" (p3). Oxford historian Stephen Howe (1999) similarly asserts: "Afrocentricism... the real aim some seem to pursue is to present not a scholarly approach...but something more akin to a new religion" (p.227). Mary Lefkowitz (1996) states: "today not everyone knows what extreme Afrocentrists are doing in their classrooms" (p. 1). David Horowitz (2007) claims that Afrocentrism "is not intellectual diversity and it is not education; it is indoctrination" (p.79). Stanley Crouch (1996) argues: "Afrocentrism is another of the clever but essentially simple-minded hustles... sweetened by gushes of pitying or self-pitying syrup" (p.77). Interestingly, Stephen Howe (1999), a fellow critic also criticized the glaring inconsistencies of Lefkowitz's work: "perhaps the most serious flaw in her book, however, is that its analysis of Afrocentric writings is almost as narrowly based as those of Hughes or Schlesinger" (p.11). Indeed, the Pulitzer Prize author, and historian Arthur Schlesinger (1992), called Afrocentricity "voodoo methodology" (p.160) and "fantasies of a glorious past (p.90). Professor of history, Tunde Adeleke's (2009) book: *The Case against Afrocentrism*, opens up with a chapter called 'Afrocentric Essentialism', which according to Tillotson (2011) places him squarely "dragging old sets of bones from one grave to another" (p.168). It is important to clarify some of the fundamental errors and misunderstandings held by these academic scholars. Asante (1988, 1990, 1998 2000, 2004, 2018), as a leading Afrocentric theorist, does not promulgate a centering of self that is neither, racist or reactionary. Indeed, "for the African to assert his or her own agency is not a racist act, but a profoundly anti-racist act" (2007, p.6). There is no universalism within the Afrocentric paradigm as its pluralistic push remains a dominant tenet on respecting other non-hegemonic ways of viewing the world, Hilliard, (1992); Nobles, (2017). Kamautu Ashanti (2003) asserts "The fact that African-centred educators often write about pluralizing the curriculum reflects the non-oppressive and counter-hegemonic nature of Africentric education" (p.9).

Appiah (2010) suggests that Afrocentrism, is framed within a homogenizing of group experiences for African people. Unanimism negates the possibility that scholars in the field do not recognize the micro aspects to Africans in Cuba, Puerto Rico, Ghana, London, Brazil, Nigeria, Sweden, Australia, and so on. These critics appear to move seamlessly from unanimism as though they were synonyms into the notions of essentialism:"It is often used as a term of opprobrium by Appiah and others when the critics fear any discussion of ontological bases for culture" (Asante, 2009, p.3).

According to Myers (2012), this is an old argument: 'The notion of African or other non-Western peoples asserting their right to formulate knowledge based upon their particularities, continues to be dismissed as essentializing-an irony and contradiction Western intellectual history has been privileged enough to escape' (p.72).

Why is it that people who practice Judaism are not therefore, considered essentialist, nor are Asians who practice their many forms of cultural production? "There is a long list of groups who proudly broadcast their racial and ethnic essence without the essentialist claim being rained upon them" (Tillotson, 2011, p.169). Indeed, Asante (1998) writes: "it is clear from my own study of history that cultures do exist and in fact persist for centuries with many basic characteristics hardly changed.. thus while I may answer to being an essentialist, I am not an immutabilist" (p.13).

Another unifying theme for the critics of Afrocentricity (Howe, 1999; Walker, 2001; Adeleke, 2009; Schlesinger, 1992; Crouch, 1996; Appiah, 2010) is in regard, to their singular, consistent and collective misuse of the word 'Afrocentrism'. Leading scholars (Mazama, 2002, Karenga, 1986, 2002; Asante, 2007, 2018; Tillotson, 2011; Yehudah, 2015) have persistently defined the correct term as Afrocentricity.: "The term Afrocentrism was first used by opponents of Afrocentricity who in their zeal saw it as an obverse of Eurocentrism" (Asante, 2007, p.17). Afrocentrism is a label from conservative critics who see the African agenda as a movement to bring disharmony to society by raising the self-esteem of African people (Asante, 1998). Similarly, Karenga (2002) carefully articulates the distinction between the two words and cautions against the misuse of the word Afrocentrism: "'It must never be conceived of, or employed as a reaction, to or an African version of Eurocentrism, with its racist and structured denial of and deformation of the history and humanity of peoples of color" (p.77).

Are these authors deliberately misusing this term to mislead and obfuscate the central tenets of this paradigm? Are these critics, trapped within a dichotomous logic of a binarized set of realities? Or, have these critics not read thoroughly, widely and deeply enough in order that they simply appeal to popular culture and its orientation? Walker, (2001) and Crouch (1996) down-play the importance of the affective and conative domains in epistemic contexts; however, the triangulation of cognitive, affective and conative domains is essential for healthy human development (Allal & Ducrey 2000; Boyle & Charles 2013). Instead, the critics ridicule the rescuing and reclamation of African history as 'gushes of self-pitying syrup. Lefkowitz (1996) and Horowitz (2007) appear to demonstrate unsubstantiated positions in their work that border on a particularized, emotional and psychological landscape rather than a scholarly critique. "We do not need *characterization* of others from Mary Lefkowitz or any other Eurocentric scholar, what is needed, pure and simple, is *documentation.* (Hilliard, 2002, p.59, original emphasis). Even in the face of overwhelming documented linguistic, scientific and historical evidence, some of the critics display what Franz Fanon (1967) philosopher and psychologist called: cognitive dissonance: 'Sometimes people hold a core belief that is very strong; and when they are presented with evidence that works against that belief, the new evidence cannot be accepted. It would create a feeling that is extremely uncomfortable called cognitive dissonance, and because it is so important to protect the core belief, they will rationalize, ignore and even deny anything that does not fit in with the core belief' (p119).

It would be unwise to suggest that it is solely within an adult domain that cognitive dissonance is experienced. The simplistic notion that children are homogenous beings centres on the premise that if an African episteme is being taught and therefore will be automatically and uniformly received, internalised and accepted by all recipients. Pulitzer Prize winner William Raspberry (1990) contends that 'It is a questionable assumption that black children with the vaguest notions of their African ancestry can be inculcated with African culture more easily than the culture to which they are daily exposed" (p.2). This is interesting on several levels; as Raspberry (1990) infers that *all* black children will have only a 'vague notion of their African ancestry' and presumably will not try to seek this out through the different modes of classroom behaviour and ways of being that may be mislabelled as 'attitude problem', 'difficult', 'aggressive', 'limited/average' and so on. Is this because the dominant episteme is Eurocentric? Or rather, that there is no 'cultural capital at home? Or, is it, that Africanity is a negative geographical location? Raspberry (1990) does not attempt to explore the myriad reasons why some children may have no connection to their African ancestry, Sefa Dei (1996) suggests it is the negativity about Africa that schools and the popular media present alongside the teaching of episodic disconnections between the Caribbean, the Americas, North America and Africa. The strong semantic use of 'inculcation' that Raspberry (1990) has chosen is problematic for Tillotson (2011): 'Somehow, he forgets that many successful groups spend time and resources to do, what he says is not possible for African Americans. Asians, Muslims, those of Jewish faith, Italians and other groups make sure their children know their ancestral lineage, history and culture' (p.163).

Why, then, is it problematic for black children to benefit from the same model of cultural pride and self-determinism?

Let's examine the Phenomenology of Hesitation. The importance of the triangulated affective (to feel), conative (to act) and cognitive (to think) domains within an Afrocentric paradigm and formative pedagogy (i.e. the researcher's Reframed Units) have previously been discussed.

It is here, that Al- Saji's (2014) *Hesitation and Affect* within those domains gain its confluence with a phenomenology of hesitation. Simply put, they are compatible as theorized components, which support a teleological programme such as the researcher's Reframed Curriculum Units. Al-Saji (2013) asserts: 'In hesitation the phenomenological moment, and ontological structure when racializing habits of seeing can be internally fractured. It is critical to transformation. I argue, to distinguish two forms of hesitation: the paralyzing hesitation of interiorized objectification and the productive hesitation that keeps habit fluid and allows improvisation and responsivity to take place' (2013,p.1).

For Bergson (1993) hesitation defines the structure of time, the ontological interval: "time is what hinders everything from being given at once" (in Al-Saji, 2014, p.142). Bergson (1993), suggests that closure on reality, must be avoided as there is no completion, as a *being,* one is always *becoming.* How we see, feel and think is critical to our development and understanding towards the perception of melanated bodies in humanizing ways. Phenomenologically, to feel, the bodily affective response, is critical to enacting momentary and sustained hesitation. Indeed, Al-Saji (2014) argues:"The recalcitrant invisibility that structures racializing vision and affect; the "I cannot see or feel otherwise" means that antiracism[11]/antiracist practice needs to be more than a discursive/cognitive intervention" (p.142). What if my visual field; is still dominated with dehumanizing images of black bodies in the spaces that contain both socializer and socialized? How then, do I begin to recalibrate my affective, conative and cognitive responses to a mythologized, episodic history, through the teaching of hegemonic master scripts? The importance of disrupting *habitual action* is an important way forward for Al-Saji (2014), she posits, that in the necessary delays or 'hesitating effect' that are part of this paradigm and action research interventions, we must teach that "through affect the body waits before acting" (p.143). Simply put; phenomenology of hesitation has the potential to rescue and reclaim the black body from its perceived inferiorization. However, this is not a simple process, which can be 'read off and read in' as some formulaic set of bullet points, Casey (2014) reminds us that: 'Racializing perceptions proceeds at a velocity such that we cannot see it happening, faster

---

[11] Racism is a complex nexus, a cognitive architecture used to invent, re-imagine, and evolve the presumed political, social, and economic, sexual and psychological superiority of the white races in society, while materializing the imagined inferiority and hastening the death of inferior races. Said differently, racism is the manifestation of the social processes and concurrent logics that facilitate the death and dying of racially subjugated peoples (Curry, 2017, p.4).

than the speed of thought. This contributes to its apparent immediacy and its naturalizing effect' (in Al-Saji, 2014, p.147).

Professor of philosophy and phenomenology, Edward Casey (2014) calls attention to the power of the internalization of culture and the messages of culture, which have the capacity: 'If racializing affect is not deconstructed from within, its violence remains and will be displaced into other processes of 'othering' and onto racialized bodies (ibid).' This 'deconstruction from within' can only come about if we begin with Henry's (2006) 'clearing of the way' of the dominant scripts of the Hegelian school of phenomenology. This, is then, followed by the re-instituting and rescuing of 'first sight' consciousness as proposed by Du Bois (1965) in order to see oneself truly through one's own eyes.

As an empirical example of 'hesitation' from the fieldwork in which the researcher (Charles, 2019) taught a Reframed Unit called the 'Genesis of Geometry', the following encapsulates Al Saji's model (2014). In a presentation to Y3,Y4, Y5 & Y6 children, they were asked (and showed a primary resource visual of a castle), "where do you think that the first castle was built and how old do you think it is?" One hundred percent of the responses were centred geographically in Europe - Spain, England, Scotland, and, France. The researcher told the children that the first castle to be built in the world was in Nubia in the town of Buhen, (this was located and pointed out on the map), and it is over 5,000 years old. There was an audible silence in the hall until Menes, (child from sample) exclaimed: "You mean in Africa!?". All of the children in the presentation were exposed momentarily, to the phenomenology of hesitation, a moment of disruption in habitual thinking and in their organizing schema of history, identity and location. The author's' teaching programme offered through the duration of the half-term programme, opportunities, evidence and insights as alternatives to the normed curriculum that they are currently experiencing in the classroom.

Contemporary researchers such as Holloway, (1997) and Hycner, (1999) suggest limitations and criticize the traditional strict boundaries that are taken up within phenomenological research: "There is an appropriate reluctance on the part of phenomenologists to focus too much on specific steps [because] this would do great injustice to the integrity of the phenomenon" (Hycner, 1999,pp 143-144). Indeed, Lauwers (2013) calls this a 'cookbook' approach in which researchers are 'encouraged' to adopt through inculcated practices, such as strict rules, procedures and boundaries, which they must operate within. These critiques argue that it is more about researcher attitude than about methodology (Lauwers, 2013, p20). The danger in becoming a closed researcher, one who utilizes a strict adherence to steps in research methods, was stated by Fanon (1967) that 'It is good form to introduce a work of psychology with a statement of its methodological point of view. I shall be derelict. I leave methods to the botanists and mathematicians. There is a point at which *methods devour themselves' (*p.5. original emphasis*).

Fanon (1967) is explicitly cautioning against what Lauwers (2013) signals: "the danger is real when the researcher makes statements based on known scientific reference points, while the essence of the experience of the participants remains hidden" (p.20). Van Manen (1990) does not provide a formulaic, gradational specification of phenomenological research in his book: *Researching lived experience.* Rather he suggests the importance of personal experiences, which include the study of etymological source of concepts; use of interviews; protocols or observations; use of literature and art because phenomenological research is a *method without technique* (p.131 original emphasis).Van Manen (1990), appears to be contradicting his earlier statements, as phenomenology is replete with techniques. Does this framework create anxiety for the researcher? According to phenomenologist and philosopher Marilyn Ray (1994) "To attempt a phenomenological study without having knowledge of its philosophical foundations...would invalidate or severely impede a study's credibility" (p.123). Therefore, it is noteworthy, that this book is grounded etymologically, in the origins of philosophy in Africa and not Europe. Bourdieu (1977) states that phenomenology offers merely an 'occasionalist illusion' (p.81). which posits the premise that inter-personal relations are restricted to 'individual to individual' interactions. Additionally, this assumption extends into the centering sphere of 'agency' and 'voice' which views its power as emancipatory. Lauwers (2013) suggests that this "emancipatory potential is doomed to remain idealistic because by focusing only on how the participants describe a certain experience, the larger context is ignored (p.25).

However, Bourdieu (1977) argues that: "there are always wider structural constraints unconsciously informing any particular inter-action" (1977 p. 81). 'Bourdieu (1990) states that phenomenology is "mistaken in its view of society as an emergent product of decisions, actions and cognitions of conscious alert individuals to whom the world is given as immediately familiar" (p.42). Throop & Murphy (2002) criticize Bourdieu's exaggerated belief that "individuals have agency and can infuse their life-world with meaning and sense" (p.190). Simply put, Bourdieu's hierarchical view of the 'individual' is an elitist perspective. As an implication, which suggests questionable outcomes, this probes the idea of truth and fidelity as areas of concern within phenomenology. *Truth and the Rhythm of Phenomenological Research* by psychologist, Steen Halling (2010) reminds researchers, through the work of Robert Coles (1964), to question who they are personally, professionally and culturally. 'Here I am trying to give prominence to the lives of these people, to their involvements with the *world*, but there has to be *qualification:* as I have seen and known these lives and involvements' (p.34. original emphasis).
Here, Halling's (2010) research moves away from the spaces of Bourdieu's (1977) criticism of the participant and notions of truth, to the limitations and issues centered upon the researcher. How well do I understand the phenomena under study as experienced by the participants? How qualified am I in the areas that I am researching? Do I understand the complex interplay of socially mediated realities in relation to my own professional and personal common sense? This necessary probing not only questions the authenticity of research projects, also, of the fundamental importance of asking uncomfortable questions and the ability to be truthful in response. In short, "To be among those who fail to escape the cocoon of their own tradition" (Gergen, 2002, p.464), is phenomenologically suspect. Halling (2010) concludes his critique by quoting the old proverb: "Children and fools tell the truth" he then provides an updated version: "Only children and fools believe there is a truth

to be told" (p.131). Within the parameters of this book, a further iteration could now read as: "Only children who remember being children tell the truth". Simply put, it is our humanity as an embodied being which leads to greater expressions of truth.

Chapter 4: Global connections & triangles

The majority of teachers' 'historical understanding, and hence their starting point for their teaching, is inaccurate. Notably, there is no classroom material which teaches that the oldest recorded living civilization is over 30,000 years (Imhotep 2013; Barashango, 1991)

The 'Genesis of Geometry' is one Unit of the five Unit programme conceptualized, designed and written by the author. The teaching sessions related to the Unit's content are the focus of the research and the data discussed in the book was generated during those teaching sessions by the students involved.
Each of these sessions within the Units is intended to be taught as an integrated, theme-based whole in which subject discipline areas of language, history, mathematics, geography, science form the basis for student and teacher co-construction and development. A formative teaching and learning culture is one of learner-involvement based on inclusion and the strengthening of each student's affective domain [leading to conation and more effective learning].

The author utilized the formative pedagogical strategy of 'guided group' teaching and learning as the basis for ensuring learner-centred teaching sessions. This method was used in all the teaching sessions described in this book.
For those who have not come across or are not familiar with using 'guided group teaching', the following section should be helpful.

'It is a first principle for us [the authors] that if you are teaching children as a whole class group, rather than planning your teaching and learning around individual learning needs, then you cannot [claim to] be teaching formatively. If you teach without differentiation then how can you be matching learning to each child's developmental needs?' [Boyle & Charles 2008] The differentiated teaching method, which 'guided group teaching' is based up was actually nested in the 'Better Schools Report' [DES 1985] within that report's four foundation principles of teaching, namely: 'broad, balanced, relevant and differentiated'. Our classroom research-based experience over many years has confirmed our belief that using the guided group strategy in a differentiated classroom setting 'balances learning needs common to all students with more specific needs tagged to individual learners' [Tomlinson 2001, p.4]. McAdamis's research [2001] evidenced that 'Differentiation [enables] the teacher to focus on the same key principles for all students, however the *instructional process, the pace and rate towards understanding those concepts varies*' [p.3. authors' italics].

The authors define a guided group as one which always operates/functions within the normal whole-class system and pedagogical-structural intention i.e. from homogeneity to individualization. The guided session should always be planned on [1] new learning or [2] on consolidating a new concept which the teacher has reflected upon and on that reflection s/he feels that a group/perhaps more than one group of students has not internalized or [3] the session is focused on a significant objective within a series of stepped activities and the teacher feels that s/he has to audit and review those steps within a guided group session. So, how is the 'guided group' set up and managed within the classroom context. The teacher [with the teaching assistants/support staff if that model prevails in the local/national teaching system, and with the involvement of the students – who may have suggested ways of tackling the problem or learning objective] will have planned a number of differentiated learning activities [tasks] within one teaching theme [single subject/domain or integrated learning is immaterial]. Three out of the four or five groups into which the class has been sub-divided will be working independently [or with teaching assistant support] on those tasks. The group of students, who will form the first guided group session, are working with the teacher and continue to be in a face-to-face working situation with the teacher. The duration of that focused, uninterrupted, guided teaching session will be approximately 20 minutes. The teacher and her/his support staff will have pre-planned a rota of theme-related, guided group sessions to support and challenge carefully differentiated groups throughout that one day – s/he will review progress across the individuals in each group and re-format the groups according to learning progress for the next day and throughout the teaching week/sessions.

The authors see the importance of 'guided group teaching' as impactful on student learning and supplying crucial teaching evidence for the teacher. That impact can be summarized in four steps: a 'guided group' is a strategic organizational or learning management device; it is the optimal opportunity for specific, focused teaching;
the small group teaching context enables the targeted learning to be planned with maximum accessibility for both the teacher and the student; and finally, it is a critical opportunity for the teacher to focus his/her assessment observations [for example, of individual learning behaviours, contributions, etc] to a teaching group sized at no more than five students.

For the pedagogist, the theoretical underpinning of a 'guided group' teaching and learning philosophy has a number of research antecedents. Hayes [2008] evidences that student-centred teaching 'includes behaviours that actively involve [the student] in guiding the learning process, such as offering choices, encouraging activity and suggesting solutions' [p.433]. From the inception of work, initially as classroom teachers, then as researchers and analysts, the authors believe that teaching is not transmission, a 'one-way process from the teacher to the child, it is a fluid, dynamic and often a seemingly effortless dance between teacher and student' [Matthews 1999, p.162] To us, the 'guided group' context supports our opinion that effective teaching has to be a transactional partnership between student and teacher, that 'teachers and children are partners in teaching and learning transactions. We need to find ways of interacting with children to co-construct shared meanings in ways that we cannot do if the children themselves are not active participants in exploring the situation' [Makin & Whiteman, 2006, p.35]. This is the philosophy upon which the following teaching sessions are based. For example, the word geometry is understood as: Geo- (earth), metry (measurement). Linguist, historian and professor of Humanities Theophile Obenga states in his book *La Geometrie Egyptienne* (1995): Egyptian Geometry as measurement of the earth, "that is to say the art of measuring land...where the cultivated ground was shared out between the Egyptians in equal lots" (p.2). For Herodotus, an ancient Greek historian: "Geometry first came to be known in Egypt, where it was passed into Greece" (Rawlinson, 1880, p.179). Furthermore, Gadalla (2016) observes: "All Egyptian art and architecture, including representations of the human figure, followed a precise canon of proportion. This canon was also applied to Egyptian sculptures, friezes, and paintings and they were carefully planned according to harmonic, geometric and proportional laws" (p.6).

This teaching session with children across the UK primary school range of Years 3 – 5 was an exploration of carved triangles from its African genesis and the global connections of triangles [see Figures 9,10,11 below]. The classroom had a range of maps and projections as resource on display (this became a permanent feature of every session) which opened up unsolicited, personal dialogues emanating from travels made by the children: All the children's names are pseudonyms.

Hatshepsut: The countries are small (points to Mercator map) but on this map the countries are big like Africa (refers to Peter's map, figure 9 below)

Figure 9: Peter's projection map.

> Researcher: Yes, it (Peter's) is more accurate when we are talking about the world. This is Britain enlarged or 'blown up' (points to UK map) and it shows exactly where we live and all of the different counties.
> Hatshepsut: When I travelled to London on the map it looks like it could take days to get there but actually, it takes a couple of hours
> Researcher: Hatshepsut, you just said something important there about understanding 'space' (spatial awareness), and what looks much further away than what it actually is, so anytime that we talk about maths, geography, history in our learning you must always place yourself in the context of a map.
> Hatshepsut: When I am in London, I do know where I am
> Researcher: This is very important... (the rest of the group, Shaka and child 1 listened intently)

Similarly, the second group (Menes, Shane, & Michael) also began to talk about themselves in relation to the maps on display:

Researcher: So, when I put my detective glasses on and looked in one of my books the patterning suggests that the date is too late, and they look like the one in South Africa. (referring to carved triangles found in the UK, fig 10, below).

Figure10: Newgrange, Ireland

Menes: Have you been to Dubai?
Researcher (nods)
Shane: I went to Dublin when I was 6.
Researcher: How old are you now?
Shane: Seven and I stayed with my cousins when I went to Dublin
Menes: How is Dublin in Ireland?
Shane: Then I stayed in Preston (researcher and all children are listening to each other)
Researcher: Yes, (says child's name) what is your question?
Michael: When you said South Africa, it kind of looks like a triangle (stands up and points to the location on Peter's map).
Menes: Hey!!Wow!

This group were confidently sharing each other's travelling experiences, whilst still retaining and maintaining the concept of the session, even though it was momentarily, 'suspended' by Shane's personal travelling experiences. The complex interplay of agency, dialogue and affective domain engagement not only created a conducive learning atmosphere, yet equally, created a space in which the children saw themselves emerging as collective individuals (Perrenoud, 1998; Allal & Ducrey, 2000; Alexander, 2005).

The following guided group session with group 3 (Akhenaten, Bobby, Chloe & Norman) expressed similar travelling experiences:

Researcher: Wow, yes in the Blombos caves in South Africa, well remembered (says child's name) but do you know what I did when I went home, I thought hmmm why don't I show the children the same triangle that popped up in Britain where we live
Akhenaten: Do you mean in a museum? (points to Africa on Peter's map)

61

Researcher: Well not on that map (points to UK map)
(All of children stand up and move closer to look at the UK map)
Norman: Hey, my cousin lives there in Stockport (points correctly to location)
Researcher: And I live here (points to Liverpool)
Akhenaten: My friend lives there and he's called Michael
Bobby: (points to Scotland)
Researcher: That's Scotland (says child's name)
Bobby: I know, and my grandpa lives there in Scotland
Akhenaten: I've got lots of cousins in Scotland
Chloe: So have I (all the children are smiling and listening, and watching each other's movements as they interact with the maps and each other).

The utilization of geography and history as subjects of exploration, enabled the children to consciously connect themselves to the content in familial ways also. There are similar examples from across the sample groups of children:

Researcher: So, what is happening is that the human family is still making triangles from 77,000 years ago, 15,000 years ago and 5,000 years ago (points to all the physical locations on the map). Now, where do you think that this one is from? (holds up Lanarkshire stone carving figure 11) Do you see what Is happening?

Figure 11: Lanarkshire stone

Hatshepsut: My mum was in Uganda and she was working in a hospital
Researcher: How long was she there?
Hatshepsut: For a week and then another week, she saw some rats and they were massive, and she saw lots of different animals. She said she doesn't keep videos, but they all looked very interesting. I wish I could go, she said it was really hot. REALLY, REALLY, HOT! (child emphasizes temperature with voice).

The children's initial dialogic exchanges demonstrated a refutation of the theme: *I Keep on Knockin but I can't come in*, as they verbally 'knocked' and pedagogically 'entered' into the teaching and learning sessions with confidence and engagement. The authors' sessions ensured that each individual child's affective domain was recognized as essential and therefore, necessary as an aspect of their growth and was encouraged. In developing the teaching programme: 'Cultural and Historical Re-Orientation in Learning', the author had to address the following basic and fundamental questions: Where is the child in her/his learning continuum? How, can the learner, be supported in her/his learning progression? How could the author develop a programme of Reframed Units of Change, which embraced the essential tenets of multimodalities and involve the learner in a meaningful way in real time? In the teaching programme, time was spent fruitfully initially in contextualizing the children, that is, in understanding the layers of geographical orientation, temporality and chronology. In short, learners needed to be contextualized to understand the global connectedness of the human family - in this instance, through geometry. For the RUoCs to be accessible, challenging and evoke responses and involvement from the learners, key pedagogical questions needed to be resolved. In teaching and learning terms, what is the balance between transmission and transaction in this process? The challenges of transaction (which also included the author's centrally controlled and therefore limited access to the children for prior 'relationship building') were addressed through a multimodal approach, language, print, images, graphics, movement, gestures, music and sound (Kress, 2003). A multimodal approach, which is sadly absent in much current teaching. The visual impact of the RUoCs demonstrated a fresh and new way of seeing and interpreting the world. As Ausburn & Ausburn (1978b) state: "Visual literacy is what is seen with the eye and what is seen with the mind" (p.291).

The following example of dialogic scaffolding represents the importance of learner (family), multimodalities, geography and history within an African episteme:

> *Researcher:* Let's think about this question, why do we find a triangle here in South Africa (points to location on Peter's map, Figure 9 above)... and here in Scotland, Wales and Derbyshire? Let's have a think about that
> *Menes:* I know, because if there wasn't any shapes, it wouldn't exist and nobody would know how to grow...(everyone in the group is listening but looking at the map)
> *Researcher:* Possibly, let's think of why... (child 1 interrupts)
> *Michael:* I've only got one answer and it's in Scotland, because my granddad, he was in the army and he went to Scotland and he said they sent little rockets out and they went up and then down. And I think it was around here, (points to location on map showing Argyll & Bute) and they tried to shoot it into the island and when it went up it went into triangles.
> *Menes:* I think they were trying to throw them up into the Scottish Councils (he is standing next to map and reading the labels).
> *Michael :* He wasn't trying to blow up Scotland they were just testing the rockets...
> *Menes:* But miss I know why South Africa is just like a triangle, when they discovered about triangles I guess they tried... they just put them on the ground I guess, a big triangle and on the map you wouldn't be able to see what it is trying to do.
> *Researcher:* So, do you think that triangles are about trying to find your way? (Menes nods) Well, should I tell you what Min said and what he was doing with his body?

(shows the group Kemetic Min (figure 12) . **Figure12:Kemetic Min (in Temple, 2000)**

Researcher: Well, he said (starts to draw on whiteboard a 3-4-5 right triangle) the mother, the father and the child are very important.

Menes: ooohh (very excited) because that's the mother (points to line 4), that is the father (points to length of hypotenuse, 5 line) and that's the child (points to line 3).

Michael: But what happens if you have twins?

Ruby: That's the second biggest.

Researcher: Well what they/Min actually meant was that when you have your first child...(Menes interrupts).

Menes: Your first child, your second child and your third child.

Researcher: And so, Min said that triangles are so sacred that they are about the family do you see? (all children engaged and looking at the diagram of the 3-4-5 right angle triangle).

Michael: Well one of the first triangles might be from India because it looks like a triangle (points to India on the map).

Researcher: Wow! We start to see triangles everywhere.

This example illustrates the importance and integration of time, pace and child voice within the layering of conceptual understandings across the group of children. Even though I (Charles), initially posed the question: 'why do triangles appear in Africa and Britain?', the children connected this idea to their own familial knowledge; i.e. my granddad's experience in the army. This contribution at first glance, from Michael, may appear erroneous and irrelevant, when in fact, this actually created a springboard for Menes to re-connect and re-loop back to the original question posed by the researcher - through Michael's use of his closing word 'triangles'. This element of recursiveness also demonstrates that when learners have a genuine, authentic sense of agency in the teaching session/theme, they are able to show that not only are they listening intently to the teacher but crucially to each other. Was Menes' comment a nascent, burgeoning understanding of something much more profound? Consider Plutarch's lst century writings about the 3-4-5 right angle triangle in *Moralia*, Vol V:

'The Egyptians hold in high honour the most beautiful of the triangles, since they liken the nature of the Universe most closely to it. This triangle has its upright of three units, its base of four, and its hypotenuse of five, whose power is equal to that of the other two sides. The upright, therefore maybe likened to the male, the base to the female, and the hypotenuse to the child of both... '(in Gadalla, 2000, p.88).

The children's cognitive capacities in the exploration of this concept, the 3-4-5 right angle triangle, evidence another group who created an extended dialogic interplay of squaring numbers within a corrected history.

Chapter 5: Squaring numbers and their historical origins

This teaching session built upon the previous session's work in relation to triangles and their mathematical origin in ancient Kemet/Egypt. The session explored the relationship between human agency, multiplication and addition.

The children explored the origin of mathematical numbers and operational relationships (i.e. squaring, multiplication, times tables). Furthermore, they were given opportunities to be fully immersed in sessions that were grounded in the historical evidence of human populations, guiding their conceptual understandings, which were not presented as abstracted, or disconnected facts. This pedagogical process resulted in genuine displays of engagement and surprise

> *Researcher:* If that is 5, what do those squares become? (researcher draws triangle on board)
>
> *Hatshepsut:* That's the child, that's the mother, that's the father (points to all of the sides correctly).
>
> *Shaka* & Miriam: Nine.
>
> *Shaka:* Because of Pythagoras.
>
> *Researcher:* What is four squared?
>
> *Miriam:* 16... and 5 squared is 25 (children are now looking at the researcher's drawing of the right angle with 3-4-5 numbers squared and figure 14).

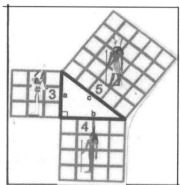

Figure 13 squaring the right angle (in African Creation Energy, 2014)

> *Researcher:* How were they able to get squares out of a triangle?
>
> *Hatshepsut:* Because they were super smart.
>
> *Researcher:* Shaka just said that it is the Pythagoras 'triple' (3-4-5)
>
> *Miriam:* Is that what it is called?
>
> *Researcher:* Pythagoras was not born then..so how can it be named after somebody who was not born yet?
>
> *Hatshepsut:* Is it a God?

Researcher: Well, they call that Pythagoras' theorem (points to figure13) . But Pythagoras was born 2,000 years ago and this is over 10,000 years old (points to pyramids and carved triangles, figure 14).

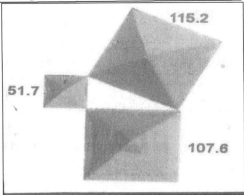

Figure 14: Ariel view of pyramids (in African Creation Energy, 2014)

Miriam: Maybe there was another Pythagoras.

Hatshepsut: Did you say that he was not born yet? How? (she looks perplexed).

Miriam: Because Pythagoras was named after the triangles.

Researcher: He was named after the triangles, but he did not create the theory.

Shaka: Maybe because nobody knew about it.

Researcher; Well they knew about it because he studied in Kemet.

Hatshepsut: How can somebody live without being born?

Researcher: Pythagoras was a Greek philosopher and he lived around 500BCE, and he is credited... (child 1 interrupts).

Miriam: What does BCE mean?

Researcher: 'Before the Current Era'... with developing Pythagoras' theorem, which is the theorem, which expresses the relationship between the heights...

Hatshepsut: Was he born in Egypt or Kemet?

Shaka: He came to Egypt when the Greeks invaded.

Researcher: Lots of students came into Egypt to study.

Hatshepsut: Oh...oh! That is what you mean by etymon, I thought you meant he wasn't born...

Researcher: If people are saying that this belongs to Pythagoras so what is happening to the knowledge...?

Shaka: Maybe because the person who made it was Egyptian but when the Greeks invaded they like took the knowledge.

Researcher: They took the information... (Shaka interrupts).

Shaka: Why don't the people actually name it after the guy who made it?

Researcher: Fantastic! What do you think about that?

Hatshepsut: It's what he needed

Shaka: So the people don't actually know the guy who made it?-(Shaka looks at the visuals as he is talking) so Pythagoras was Euclid?

Researcher: It's called the Ptah-Horus theorem (points to figure 15)

67

Figure 15: Ptah-Horus Theorem (in African Creation Energy, 2014)

Shaka; I thought that Horus was an Egyptian god?

Hatshepsut: So he (Pythagoras) was born in Greece... so people thought that he created the triangles and that he found it when they were invading Kemet.

Researcher: He studied with the master priests in Kemet to learn about the sacred triangle... he took the information back to Greece and spread the ideas as if they were...

Shaka: His.

Hatshepsut: But how did they think that it was his? How did he make it sound like it was his?

Researcher: But why do people do that?

Shaka: Because they are greedy.

Miriam: And they take credit for it.

Shaka: So most people do not know that Pythagoras did not make it...(continues to look at visuals).

Researcher: My research...(Shaka gently interrupts).

Shaka: Who is Euclid?

Researcher: He was a mathematician who studied in ancient Kemet. Euclid was said to have lived 700 years after Pythagoras and is called the 'father of geometry'. Why would he be called the 'father of geometry' when these shapes already existed?

Shaka: So, people actually thought that it was Pythagoras?

Miriam: So they took the credit.

Researcher: And they still do today.

Shaka: So most mathematicians don't know that it was actually Ptah-Horus.

Researcher: It was a whole group of priests in ancient Kemet.

Hatshepsut; So, are they a particular kind of people who created the 3-4-5 triangle? Or are they just people?

Researcher: It was named after the sacred family so all of the Master teachers...(Hatshepsut gently interrupts).

Hatshepsut: So are they like sacred people? Are they 3-4-5 people?

Researcher: They are meant to represent the whole nation to say that you are sacred, and special as a human being, and the priests recognized this.

This lengthy example of 'scaffolding' (by the researcher) and dialogic teaching demonstrates the visual, oral and aural tenets of the Phenomenology of Hesitation (Al-Saji 2004). The children, through the integration of carefully chosen texts, visuals and their own cognitive layering facilitated by the researcher, experienced not only a pedagogical moment of hesitation in their *habitual thinking*, but equally, a re-orientation in their organizing schema of history, identity and location. Interestingly, the same concept produced a different set of responses from another group who began to explore the relationship between squaring numbers and times tables all within an African episteme:

> Researcher: (draws a 3-4-5 right angle triangle on the board, figure 16) How can I make three squares out of this?

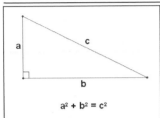

Figure 16: Right angle

> *Ptah:* (draws a 'mirror' image of the triangle and therefore completes a whole rectangle).
>
> Researcher: Good... I wasn't expecting that Ptah, but if we have the 3-4-5 triangle, how do we make 3 squares from each line? (points to a, b & c and starts to draw in a square for (a)). What is 3 squared?
>
> *All children*: Nine
>
> *Researcher*: What is 4x4?

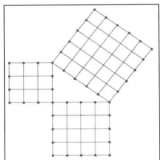

Figure17: What is squaring?

> *Zoe:* Sixteen (Researcher starts to section and draw the squares – figure 17).
>
> *Charlotte:* You have made 16 out of 4! (shows surprise).
>
> *Researcher*: Squared numbers.
>
> *Zoe*: 1,4,9,16
>
> *Charlotte*: 25 (in response to researcher drawing in 5).
>
> *Ptah*: How did you know that? (directing question to charlotte).
>
> *Charlotte* (smiles)
>
> *Zoe:* Five times table!
>
> *Charlotte*: You have done the three times table.
>
> *Bobby:* They created the times tables.
>
> *Ptah:* You mean that's what they did? (All the children are very surprised).

Researcher: This is fantastic... they made shapes (uses visuals on board as reference points), they made time-tables, and do you see how clever they were...(Ptah interjects)

Ptah: I think that Bobby should be in Y6.

Bobby: And I am the smallest person here... (smiles).

Charlotte: When they discovered triangles did they think of squares and then of times tables...? It makes sense.

Researcher: That's what they did, Charlotte everything makes sense. Everything is related, everything is connected.

The human aspect of knowledge origination is extremely important for learners of any age in any learning space. When the 'face' of the origin and location of knowledge acquisition is absent from curriculum planning and lesson content; it has the potential to slowly undermine and negate the positive psychological facility of black identity (Nobles, 2010, 2015, 2017; Wilson, 1991, 1993). Conversely, what does this paradigm create in the minds of non-black children? Gordon (2006) reminds the reader that we treat our theories as if they always existed in some sort of abstracted fashion without any human hand in its inception. In a similar vein, many educators either remove the expressed articulation of human creation from their subject teaching, which often creates a Eurocentric assumption in the minds of both teacher and learner. Or, many simply ignore the African genesis of the concept being explored because the process has created an axiological hierarchy within those cultural spaces. Psychologist Wade Nobles (2017) poses a very serious question in relation to pedagogical pursuits and axiology: "What does it mean to be human - to walk in the world as a unique, valuable being with an African face?"

Furthermore, what if the starting point of my identity is always centred around slavery, servitude and colonialism? What are the implications of a teaching profession that is 92% white? What does this do to my emerging identity and sense of humanity in an environment in which my consciousness is over dependent on how others see me? (Hegel,1910). The evidence discussed in chapters1, 2, and 3 of this book regarding the anthropological, linguistic, archaeological and historical evidence supports Nobles (2017) assertion that: 'This irrefutable evidence secures our fundamental grounding of what it is to be human, not as late comers but as progenitors, which is a much larger, profound identity' (opening segment of lecture).

The children in the above examples explored the origin of mathematical numbers and operational relationships (i.e. squaring, multiplication, times tables). Furthermore, they were given opportunities to be fully immersed in sessions that were grounded in the historical evidence of human populations, guiding their conceptual understandings, which were not presented as abstracted, or disconnected facts. This pedagogical process resulted in genuine displays of engagement and surprise; in simple terms, these lessons were over 45 minutes long with no negative behavioural issues present.

Chapter 6: Physics, concentric circles and the earth

Physics, concentric circles and the Earth

This session explored the global connections of ancient stone carved concentric circles in relation to physics and their connection to human relationships. The visuals depicting the concentric circles carved on the stones supplied a mental link to trigger the children's conceptual understanding. Therefore, the judicious use of visuals through a multimodal approach has the potential and capacity to tap into and trigger children's interests in which, communication occurs through different but synchronous modes (Kress, 2003). The session demonstrates the importance for children/learners of a judicious inter-play and complex integration of the modes of language, print, graphics, images, movement, gesture and texture. These synchronous modes form an empirical definition of multimodality to scaffold learning: 'a multimodal approach that looks beyond language to all forms of communication' (Jewitt et al 2009).

This approach highlights the potential complex interactions between media, modes and semiotic resources. The basis of our discussion of this session is that for learners, communication [whether in the forms of dialogue or the more advanced learning process of dialogic] occurs through different but synchronous modes. Over the past fifteen years or so, the learning interactions between teachers and pupils have changed in significant ways but in the main have also remained the same in non-formative ways. Children's classroom experiences within a pedagogical style which is tuned to 'performance outcomes' are still based on mono-modality (Boyle & Charles, 2013; Wyse et al 2007; Goouch 2008) and on a didactic pedagogy (Alexander & Flutter 2009). Through the researcher's conceptualization and establishing a well-planned multimodal learning environment which enabled the children to experience a range of different modes of active involvement, children, who had previously been labelled as 'disinterested' and/or 'disruptive' became intrinsically motivated and involved in their own learning. The authors' sessions were based on the needs and interests of the children as a part of their individual, differentiated learning styles and pace[s] enabling and supporting those groups of individuals to naturally develop.

This session explored the global connections of ancient stone carved concentric circles in relation to physics and their connection to human relationships.

Researcher: (The earlier part of the session had discussed the stone artifacts)

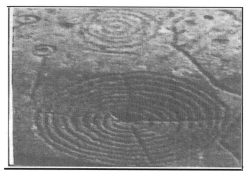

Figure 18 :carved stone Switzerland

Figure 19:carved stone Gabon-Africa

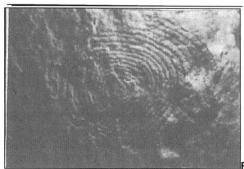

Figure 20: carved stone Newgrange-Ireland

Now, look at this (shows photo of earth's protective/ atmospheric layers). These are called the concentric circles of the Troposphere, Stratosphere, Mesosphere, Thermosphere and Exosphere. They are the layers that surround the earth, and like a blanket, that protects the earth. Have you heard of the ozone layer?

Ptah: That's why you can still feel the heat but some of the force field is like y'know the last one (points to the last layer on earth photo, fig. 18).

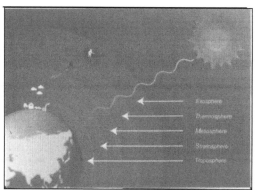

Figure 21: Earth's protective layers

Researcher: I'm going to write that on the board because that is so clever what you just said - 'the layers protect the force field'. What I would like you to do now, because everyone is sitting so nicely is to listen...this afternoon I was watching you all play in the playground, and I spotted Ptah being like a big brother and it was lovely. You were protecting Akhanaten and you were stopping a fight.

Ptah: He's my cousin you know.

Researcher: I didn't know that and you were being very protective of him like the protective layers here (points to photo of earth's layers).

Shane: And Charlotte and Menes.

Researcher: You see this is how our ancestors and the human family behaved. It was all about protecting the family and that's what Ptah was doing. Just like these atmospheric layers, he was protecting Akhanaten like a blanket and I thought how special is that. So glad that you told me that sentence Ptah, so you know all about those protective layers. So, what I would like you to do is tell me what is happening here on this sheet (shows the group the earth picture).

Bobby: Vibrating.

Researcher: And these are (points to atmosphere layers) what Ptah was doing in the playground.

Shane: Like a blanket (all of the group start to work on their sheet, general discussion between the children themselves).

Ptah: It's like the energy of the sun comes in really fast and the last layer is to protect the earth... (leans over and starts explaining to Shane that Mars has protective layers).

Researcher: Tell me more...would you like to go up?

Ptah: Kind of... at the same time yes and the same time no. Because of the risk and eventually the earth is going to just go... the sun is going to burn and I think that each year the sun is moving closer to earth and that's why they are trying to find out about Mars and trying to get everyone to Mars.

Researcher: For people to live on? It may not happen in our life time...

Ptah: No, no, not in our lifetime like when we are all dead (children start finishing their work and talking in general).

Bobby: I've got a cylinder stone at home.

Ptah: I've actually got hundreds of stones in my garden.

Gina: When I was in Russia, I told my two friends that there was a wall with lots of shapes on it and they said they are not very special. So, I said 'when we get back to (says precise regional location), I will show you that triangles and circles are very important'.

Ptah: When I crack open my stones with a little hammer I like to find if I can discover anything that is hiding in there that no-one else has found. So, each day I come home with my hammer and look and see very carefully unusual things and I've got a microscope.

Bobby: I've got a magnifying glass.

Ptah: Well a microscope is better for seeing really small things.

The authors introduced elements of physics through an Africana episteme with its interconnectedness between nature and our cosmic connection as *One*. Specifically, this relates to our human ability to nurture and to protect which is mirrored through the universe's/cosmos concentric vibrations (Coleman,1991). Clinical psychologist Edward Bynum (2012) in his book: *Dark Light Consciousness* asserts:

'An electromagnetic wave moves around the Earth's surface, reflecting on and off the ionosphere above in a serpentine motion...beneath our detachment from the earth in modern life, there is a deeper connection with our bodies to the dynamics and geodynamics of the Earth itself. These coiling, rotational, geo-dynamics are reflected in the spiralling energies of our psycho-spiritual reality...' (pp. 9 & 115).

Did the introduction of this phenomenon as presented by Bynum (2012) and expressed through an Africana episteme, enable the researcher to refute the labelling by the class teacher (see fieldwork note below) of Ptah's perceived bad behaviour and lack of cognitive abilities?

> "Well he is not a bright as Shaka but he clowns around for attention, mumbles deliberately, drops things on the floor for attention and has a bad attitude towards learning and to adults" (Field notes, October, 2018).

In our teaching sessions (that is, in the lessons that he was able to attend through not being excluded from by the school's disciplinary regime), Ptah exhibited the opposite of the class teacher's verdict [above] of 'bad attitude towards learning'. Indeed, the dialogic transcript that features Ptah (above) evidences a young learner totally engaged in the subject of physics and crucially, his connection as an inquisitive, caring and articulate human being: "I look for tiny creatures that no-one has ever found".

Ptah was revealing facets of his personality, his interests, and his capacity for social interactions (i.e. he carefully explained activity on Mars to a peer). He also demonstrated his ability to lead, instigate and co-construct lesson content openly and respectfully with the researcher and his peers. "Self-regulated learning is the fusion of skill and will" (McCombs & Marzano,1990, in Paris & Paris, 2002, p.98). The researcher did not know that Ptah was interested in geology: "I crack open my stones to discover and find things that no-one else has found...I use my microscope" as this information was not revealed in his semi-structured interview, nor would this be expected as it takes time for pupils and teachers to form 'confiding' relationships. However, also, the visuals depicting the concentric circles carved on the stones supplied a mental link to trigger Ptah's conceptual understanding. Therefore, the judicious use of visuals through a multimodal approach has the potential and capacity to tap into and trigger children's interests in which, communication occurs through different but synchronous modes (Kress, 2003).

The same lesson theme; was explored with another of the sample's guided groups. In this group was Akhanaten, a black boy from Year 3 who was consistently described as 'problematic' by his class teacher and the Head teacher:

> _Researcher:_ (motions with two hands) You see these vibrations, why would they carve them in the stone?
> _Akhanaten:_ Because they look like that (points to the Earth visual, fig. 22).

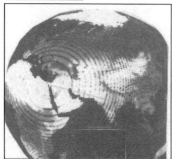

Figure 22: Earth's vibrations

Researcher: Why?

Akhanaten: It's like a special circle.

Researcher: Concentric circles.

Susan: Maybe it's one of the Indians or Brazilians or the Australians? It could mean something to the world.

Akhanaten: They look like stairs that you walk up.

Researcher: I'm going to write that on the board - well done you two!

Susan: A symbol that means something to the world.

Researcher: hmmm... they look like steps (Akhanaten interjects)

Akhanaten: But miss, it's my brother's birthday...

Researcher: (draws children back by motioning with two hands vibrations- children begin to copy)

Akhanaten: It's like a magnet.

Charlotte: So you have north and south and you try to put them together but...

Akhanaten: They repel.

Susan: Repel and retract.

Researcher: (nods) I need to work on what Susan said before: 'they are important... '(Charlotte interjects)

Charlotte: To the world.

Researcher: (Points back to magnetic field picture, fig. 18). It protects the world. When all the children are in the playground, there are some people that you move towards and there are some people that you like, some people you don't mind and some people you don't like.

Susan: Why?

Akhanaten: It's their personality and how they look.

Charlotte: It doesn't matter how they look.

Akhanaten: They are still special.

Researcher: Do you see what Akhanaten said, 'it is your personality'…Our ancestors knew that we give off a vibration and sometimes we move towards... (Susan interrupts)

Susan: We put down our scent because that's what dogs do - other dogs put down that scent and then other dogs know.

Akhanaten: Well done Susan!.

Researcher: Sometimes when I am with my friends, they give off an energy like the Earth -there are some people who don't have very nice energies, and there are some people with lovely energies.

Charlotte: Like me.

Akhanaten: So do you (points to researcher- she smiles back at him).

Charlotte: Some people get upset because another person makes them upset.

Akhanaten: It's not their fault they are upset, it's the other person.

Charlotte: It's nobody's fault it's the Devil's.

Researcher: Well, I don't know about that...but sometimes we have to take responsibility for doing right.

Charlotte: Sometimes one side of your head is saying 'do it, do it' and the other side is saying 'don't do it, it's not kind'.

Akhanaten: It's like when you are lying, you can lie about, you can say like 'I am not coming to your birthday' and you actually do, so it's just like a surprise.

Researcher: Thank you... (points back to visuals) so let's remember what Susan said at the very beginning of the session...sound waves.

Akhanaten: Magnets and footsteps.

Researcher: Good, yes, our ancestors were drawing these concentric circles so that *YOU* would get closer to *You* in order to understand yourself....

It is important to note that when I went to collect him for this session, Akhanaten was excluded from his classroom for 'bad behaviour,' and had spent most of the morning's 'teaching time' in the corridor. When he finally arrived 10 minutes late for our session, he sat down and immediately said:

"At home I did a triangle"

Researcher: You mean from last week? (he nods and smiles).

Akhanaten: I can make it into a 3-4-5 (Researcher directs him to Susan's comment that opened up the lesson).

This transcript shows how the researcher had focused the content of the session in relation to the whole child, i.e. their physical, emotional, intellectual and spiritual development. ('W)holistically' speaking, the children's positive co-construction examples enabled the successful integration of *themselves* into the subject domains. Consider the use of the words, vibrations, energies, and the ascension of moral behaviour as steps/stairs. Within an Africana episteme, King & Swartz (2018) call this a 'reclamation of cultural heritage' in which the conscious recovery of African history, culture and identity is grounded in cosmology, ontology, and axiology" (p.28). Indeed, this quest for 'wholeness' is a call for a new historiography of location (Asante, 2009; Kuhn, 1979, Carruthers 1999). To separate the mind from the body (Cartesian duality) in relation to the current schooling context as observed by Archer (2008): "constructions of the 'ideal pupil' in which the academic (configured as the 'mind') is separated off from the non-academic as signified by the Black, sexualized, working-class body (p.96) is the antithesis of ancient Kemetic teachings: 'To unify one's consciousness with the universe... and Ma'at (a deity of truth, justice, balance, order harmony, cosmic law and righteousness) and be a holistic (mind, body and soul) blend of theory and practice' (Zulu, 2012, p13).

Plato himself in his book *Laws,* written in 360BCE, discusses the importance of education in Kemet/Egypt and how those teachings and systems, made human beings more human. Did this reframed unit create a paradigmatic shift to enable Akhanaten to access DuBois' first sight consciousness? Was he seeing himself through his own eyes? Did this pedagogical style allow Charles (2019) to phenomenologically, return his mind and body back to him as Yancy's (2014) elevator scenario in positive terms, no longer as a static racial template? The evidence strongly suggests in the affirmative.

Chapter 7: Concentric circles, people and pyramids

In this session, concentric circles (2D and 3D dimensional shapes), were explored within their geographical locations and their human agency. The group had been discussing the Bulgarian gold artifact, figures 23 and 24 [below].

Transcript of session segment:

Menes: Well miss y'know .Egyptians.. it looks like when they get their families and carve it and then close it (referring to Sarcophagus), it looks like their ancestors.

Researcher: Possibly... I never thought about that Menes.

Chloe: Is it like they've carved people in gold from like when we looked at the world from smallest to biggest (has made a connection to the magnetic field image from last week's session).

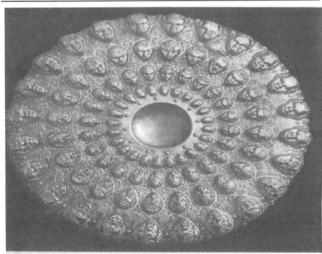

Figure 23:Bulgarian Gold phile (source, http://gettyimages.co.uk)

Researcher: Chloe well done! You have made a connection to the vibrations of the earth (all children in the group are silently absorbed, looking at the

Figure 24:close up of Bulgarian phile/ faces.
(source, http://gettyimages.co.uk)

gold image that we were learning about last week. (Researcher brings photo of Imhotep, figure 25, over to the group). Now this man was a

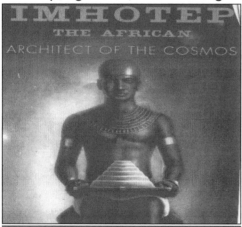

Figure 25: Book by Bauval & Brophy (2013) Illustration by Omar Buckley

great architect and he was real but he is no longer alive.

Shona: He's passed away.

Researcher: And he was from Kemet thousands of years ago and his name is... (Menes interjects)

Menes: Imhotep (pronounces correctly) is he African?

Researcher: (nods) Imhotep... and he built the stepped pyramid.

Menes: You mean he told the pharaoh to tell his workers?... you mean he was the first one to know about pyramids? And that's when triangles were created?

Researcher: Yes... good... he is the architect Imhotep.

James: We are going to make pyramids out of clay.

Researcher: Well before we do that, I just need to tell you that they (points to pyramid) were found in Britain.

Menes: WHAT!!! (rest of children have a surprised look on their face).

Researcher: In Wiltshire (goes over to map to point out location of Wiltshire).

Chloe: So it's still like in Britain?

<u>Shona</u>: No, it's not in Manchester (corrects Menes).
<u>*Researcher*</u>: (Shows the picture of pyramid at Silbury, fig 26).

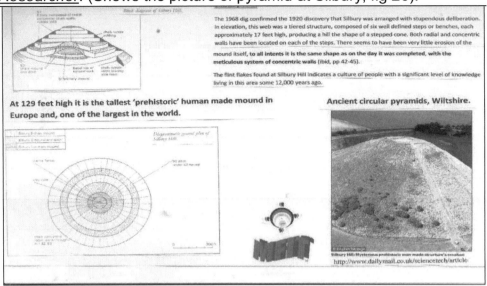

Figure 26: Silbury Hill in Dames (1976)

<u>*Chloe*</u>: So the people travelled to it and said 'hey this looks like a pyramid but it doesn't have a triangle on the top bit because it has circles.'
<u>*Researcher*</u>: It doesn't look like a pyramid because they have covered it in grass.
<u>*Shona*</u>: Is that because they don't want people to find it?
<u>*Researcher*</u>: Why would they put grass on it?
<u>*Shona:*</u> Is it because if people knew they would tell the museum and... (stops and gets muddled).
Researcher: Well, the museum does know that it's there... (Sally interjects).
<u>*Sally:*</u> Well I think that they covered it in grass because when it wasn't covered in grass the pyramid looked very tacky and old and it didn't look presentable and the other option is that people might find it and climb it and get to the top and say ' I believe I can fly'.

This teaching transcript shows how each learner was able to make a conceptual connection with the material and visuals from a sequential cognitive standpoint. Which meant that (the researcher), was providing the human visual element of geometry to the children i.e. through the use of primary source artefacts. Therefore, Chloe was able to articulate through observation, the link between physics and technology: "They've carved people in gold like when we looked at the world - from smallest to biggest". This concentricity of thought as a higher order skill; was being formulated in the mind of the learner, and then being expressed to other learners in a conducive, open learning environment. The co-constructed element of this dialogue encouraged Sally, after remaining silent for most of the opening session, to make a conative connection with physics, self and a circular pyramid:"People may find it, and climb it, and get to the top and say: 'I believe I can fly'. Professor of History and Africana Studies Oba T'Shaka (2001) states: "Through concentric thought we ascend the spiral ladder of transformation through the cycles of life, rising to the level of perfection where the body becomes one with the soul" (2001, p.1). Was Sally demonstrating a nascent understanding and connection with the soul as described by T'Shaka? Or was she simply expressing a child-like desire to jump off something high? Interestingly, John Dewey (1902) in his seminal text *The Child and the Curriculum* discussed the importance of education as a whole, and not as "disconnected facts torn away from their original place in experience and rearranged with reference to some general principle" (p.6). He urged teachers to view the "universe as fluid and fluent; its contents dissolve and reform with amazing rapidity" (ibid). Dewey recognized the importance of the child as central in the teaching and learning process:

'Subject matter can never be got, into the child from without... it involves reaching *out of the mind*. Literally, we must take our stand with the child and the departure from him. It is he and not the subject- matter, which determines both quality and quantity of learning' (p.9, emphasis added).

Dewey's (1902) dominant and singular use of the patriarchal pronoun 'he/him' throughout his text detracts from the need for gender balance within the learning process. However, this should not negate Dewey's (1902) emphasis on methodological child-centeredness with the teacher using the child's (learner's) input to enable the cognitive layering of concept formation. Put simply the child must have an active and dominant role in knowledge construction to enable progress towards automaticity to be achieved by that/each child/learner.

Did this methodology enable Menes to articulate a similar level of recursiveness for example, like Chloe's connection with a previous session? As, Menes stated: "You mean he (Imhotep), told the Pharaoh to tell his workers...? You mean he was the first to know about pyramids, and then, that's when triangles were created?" Here, Menes is in triplicate, explicating Dewey's (1902) 'mind from within'. He has retained the lesson content from several sessions back and is applying it in the new context as a catalogue file in his "executive function memory (EF) defined as the cognitive abilities that consciously support goal-directed behaviours" (Ackerman & Friedman-Krauss, 2017, p.1). In this pedagogical process of incorporating the aspects of Merleau- Ponty's (1968, 2002) phenomenology of embodiment, I was able to "rescue every voice" to reveal each child as a learner with agency, space and intelligence.

The children from another of the guided group sessions exhibited a different set of cognitive and dialogic layering. The lesson was over 55 minutes in duration therefore, in order to capture the pattern of knowledge construction by the children, a large section of the session is cited necessarily. The dialogue transcript that follows is a powerful example of the phenomenology of hesitation (Al-Saji, 2004).

Researcher: Now here is the architect (shows front cover of the book: 'Imhotep the African Genius, figure 25).
Miriam: You mean he designed that pyramid? (surprise in voice).
Researcher: Yes, he did ...what does he have around his neck?
Shaka: Circles.

Miriam: But they are semi-circles because it goes behind his neck...is the pyramid that size? (refers to model of pyramid on Imhotep's knee).

Researcher: No, the pyramid was huge in real life (shows the photo of the stepped pyramid to show the scale and a person standing next to it, figure 27).

Figure 27 :stepped pyramid

Hatshepsut: We were learning about miniatures last week.

Researcher: Good and this week we are learning about... (Miriam interjects).

Miriam: The big ones.

Hatshepsut: So each week we learn a different subject.

Researcher: Well, yes, but I also want you to understand that these ancient communities really understood about measurements so... if you can build tiny, you can build big (Shaka interjects).

Shaka: So how old is the stepped pyramid?

Researcher: It is approximately 5,000 years old (Shaka continues).

Shaka: And those ones? (points to Nsude pyramids, fig 28)

Figure 28 : Nsude Pyramids (source: The Rainbow (2017) who built the Igbo pyramids? http:www.thenigerianvoice.com/news/259458/who-built-the-igbo-pyramids-mysteries-yet-to-be-unraveled.html

Researcher: Well, we don't have a date for those... but we know that they are old...

Miriam: Couldn't they use what they know to work out the date?

Researcher: They could, but what would happen if they find out that they are older than the Stepped pyramid?... what's going to happen to our thinking?

Hatshepsut: It will change.

82

Researcher: And sometimes people don't want to change your thinking which is not good... and you have to keep being challenged with your thinking this is very important...

Miriam: I'm trying to think how old the Nigeria pyramids are..

Researcher: Ok, (says child's name) what is going to happen if people think that Nigeria has older pyramids.. (Shaka interjects)

Shaka: That Nigeria built the first ever pyramids.

Researcher: And what is that going to do with your thinking?

Hatshepsut: It will change it and everyone will start to think that they took the idea from Nigeria.

Researcher: Yes, a bit like Pythagoras, do you remember our discussion this week about him? (all the children nod).

Shaka: So people don't want other people to know that Nigeria built the first pyramids?

Researcher: It's a possibility, so as a researcher I have to keep pushing back this information in my mind... to say, 'hmmm that doesn't sound right'.

Miriam: So, do you think there are other pyramids in Africa?

Researcher: What a great question... I think that the whole of Africa was one cultural unit and they were all sharing information together. It wasn't like one was doing that (points to different parts of Africa on map) and this in isolation... they were travelling and communication across the whole continent. My research is showing that...

Shaka: But how did they build it that high? (points to Stepped pyramid photo, fig 28)

Researcher: Well, Shaka what they built was scaffolding and I have a book at home that shows the ancient Kemetic people with scaffolding and they could actually climb (Shaka interjects).

Shaka: So, once they built the first layer they would climb up and build the second layer but how did they climb down? Oh, I know...

Researcher: Ok... this is in Britain (shows Silbury Hill photo, figure. 26) and this is going to push back your thinking... this is Silbury Hill found in Wiltshire- Shaka can you find it on the map? (Shaka locates it very quickly).

Hatshepsut: You mean we can actually go there!?

Researcher: (nods).... and so I discovered in one of my books that if you take the grass off, guess what is underneath?

Hatshepsut: Stones... chalk.

Researcher: (shows picture of Hill without grass) What does it look like?

Miriam: ITS A PYRAMID!!! (shocked and surprised)

Researcher: Yes, good Miriam.

Shaka: You mean they buried this pyramid? (very surprised in voice)

Researcher: Yes, buried with green grass, so why would people cover up Britain's pyramid?

Hatshepsut: Noooo idea!

Shaka: Maybe they didn't want us to know that Britain built the first ever pyramid.

Researcher: So they built them here and here (points to different locales on the African continent). I had to buy this special book to find the picture of the hidden design of the hill. Look its 129 ft children!! Look at the tiny car at the bottom of the hill to show how HUGE this pyramid is! HUGE....

Miriam: How big is 129 feet?

Researcher: It's taller than this whole school. In fact, (takes children over to the window to show a neighbouring block of flats as a comparator) it's as big, as tall and as wide as that building.

Hatshepsut: WHAT!!!!! (All children are surprised)

Shaka: How did they build it?

Miriam: Did they take the measurements from the pyramid of Egypt?

Researcher: Super! ... So what does that tell you about the people?

Miriam: That they knew about this (points to Nsude pyramids, figure 28) and they knew about that (points to Stepped pyramid, figure 28).

Researcher: And in one of my books, the scientist says that it is 12,000 years old, which makes it older than Kemet and Nigeria... How is that possible?

Miriam: This could be the first pyramid... and I thought that it was always in Egypt.

Researcher: So what am I doing to your thinking?

Hatshepsut: Changing it and pushing it...

Researcher: Back and changing our understanding of dates and making you think about the first people.

Hatshepsut: Is that the only one in Britain or are there more?

Researcher: What a great question - Shaka put that back on the stand for me - thank you (puts photo of Hill away)

Hatshepsut: Are they all under hills?

Researcher: Yes, many of them are all under hills, good, Hatshepsut.

Miriam: With grass on top?

Hatshepsut: Why are people burying them?

Researcher: Well, let's look at this one as it was found in.. (Miriam interjects)

Miriam: How do people find them? Do they bury them again after they find them?

Researcher: Yes, after they were discovered they were buried again.

Miriam: But how do we know about it? Did they dig it up?

Researcher; Great question Miriam- previous researchers… remember how we talked about how information gets passed on...?

Miriam: Oh yes, they tell each other.

Researcher: And how old history books have the original photographs, so this is an original photograph (points to source photo of Marlborough Mound, figure 29

_____

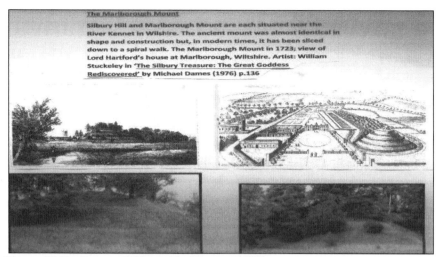

Figure 29 Marlborough Mound in Dames (1976)

All the children begin to ask who? where? when? all at once). Well, listen carefully to this information. This is covered in grass and a layer of the pyramid was cut away to make it look smaller. Now, I'm giving you a lot of information here and I would like you to just stop for a minute or two and think about what is here (children still asking which is the oldest etc). So, we know that (points to Africa, Britain on the map) we are all connected, as we have pyramids in Kemet/Egypt, Nigeria and Britain and there are others throughout the world...

Hatshepsut: Are there at least one in all of the continents?

Researcher: Yes, that's an important way of looking at it, Hatshepsut. Now does anyone have anything floating in their heads that may be a little confusing? (Hatshepsut answers 'yes') I'll come back to you, Hatshepsut. (there is a silence for about 8 seconds). Shaka, any questions? (shakes head), Ok, so what we have are pyramids rising all around the world. (Shaka interjects)

Shaka: Do people still build pyramids today?

Researcher: No, because the precise technology has been lost and Imhotep (points to picture, figure. 25) he was a master architect.

Miriam: But how do we know what he looked like?

Researcher: Great question Miriam. Well, where he was from (points to map - Men Nfer – Memphis, Near Cairo) and the artist looked at the people from this place.

Shaka: Almost like their relatives or something like that.

Researcher: That's right, like their ancestors.

Hatshepsut: Ok, I'm confused... how long did it take to cover the Hill (referring to Silbury).. to cover the pyramid?

Researcher: They started approximately two hundred years ago

Hatshepsut: So they started to cover it 200 years ago?

Miriam: When did they finish doing it?

Researcher: It's already finished, the grass is there... and we know that it started 200 years ago because of this research (points to book), but we don't know when it was finished.

Shaka: Was it discovered in 1920?

Researcher: The 1968 discovery confirmed the 1920 discovery (reading information from visual resource) and I hope that one day when you drive past it you might say 'ah I know what's underneath it'...

Hatshepsut: A pyramid.

Shaka: But they covered it up, and most people don't know that there is a pyramid there

Researcher: Yes, and you are the first children to know maybe in the whole of Britain ? (All the children are smiling).

Miriam: So where is it again? (Shaka points to location on map to show her)

Researcher: So you are part of some very important research children.

Hatshepsut: So every big hill I see, there might be a pyramid underneath?

Researcher: Well, you never know Hatshepsut...Now (then researcher begins to explain next activity).

The children, in this example of dialogic layering, were enabled, through the use of scaffolding and multimodalities to move beyond, as Al-Saji (2014) argues: "the recalcitrant invisibility that structures racializing vision and affect" (p.142). Through the reframed teaching unit, linked with an understanding of Al-Saji's (2014) critique of a myopic antiracist approach, typically dominated by a discursive and cognitive intervention, the author presented a new strategy, which broadened both the child's visual field and affective domain. In calling for a new historiography of experience (Asante, 1990, 1998, 2000; Karenga, 2003; Mazama, 2003; King & Swartz, 2018), this example demonstrates how interrupting habitual thinking, can be utilized through the application of phenomenology of hesitation (Al-Saji, 2014). In short, the children were (seeing, feeling and thinking), and being exposed to the importance of time, and on the non-closure of reality in the process of *becoming*.

Therefore, to see the image of Imhotep, the acknowledged multi-genius architect, as a melanated body created a 'hesitating affect' evidenced in Miriam's comment: "How do we know that he looked like that?" In broadening her visual field, her question, which was posed almost at the end of the session (although the image was viewed at the beginning of the session), suggests that she was now in the process of recalibrating her affective, conative and cognitive responses to a new historiography of experience. Was this the first time, in which a melanated historical figure, had ever been shown to her in such positivity? It is interesting to note that the children (as shown by their questions) were very keen to know the dates of the pyramid constructions. This, then, allowed (the researcher), to pose a semi-quandary: "Well, we don't have a date for those (Nsude pyramids, fig.23) but we know that they are old". This then lead Miriam to answer the probe with sound reasoning: "Couldn't they use what they know to work out the date?". (Miriam was referring to carbon 14 and thermo-luminescence (TL) techniques). In response to this section of dialogue within the session, (the researcher) began to layer and disrupt habitual thinking: "They could but what is going to happen if they find out that they are older than the Stepped pyramid? - what is that going to do to our thinking?" Hatshepsut replied with "It will change" in parallel with Shaka's response: "That Nigeria built the first ever pyramids" to which

Hatshepsut's conjecture confirms:"change and everyone will start to think that they took the idea from Nigeria".

The children, in this session were immersed within a new historiography of experience utilizing a simple, yet judicious use of integrative probes, which presented Africa as a unified progenitor rather than as a passive recipient in waiting (for Europeanization). The children then began to enter into the learning/research process as engaged participants demonstrating their reasoning, sequential thinking and active problem solving and being systematic in their deductions; this contrasts to the predictable transmission of the recitation script observed in too many classrooms currently. This is evidenced by Miriam asking a simple but very important question: "So do you think there are other pyramids in Africa?". Not only has she conceptually, spatially and in her orientation, moved beyond Egypt but she in one semantic stroke has unified the continent by naming it Africa. Monges (1997) urges that we reconstitute the head back on Africa to restore the dislocations and disorientations that colonialism has instituted. I conceptualised a paradigm shift in thinking for the children through the context of teaching a continuum of black achievement within the Reframed Units.

In short, in utilising these visual evidences, (the researcher) presented the globality of the human family as black in origin (i.e. through examples such as pyramid building) to enable the children to recognize and connect to the development of that human family in the United Kingdom (see Chapter 1: Human Family Origins). The surprise, disbelief and excitement when the children discovered that there are pyramids in the UK was exemplified by Miriam's "IT'S A PYRAMID!" When the researcher revealed that it had been covered in grass, Shaka's questioning revealed the necessary 'delays' in habitual thinking: "You mean they buried this pyramid?!" followed by " Maybe they didn't want us to know that Britain built the first ever pyramid". Sullivan & Tuana (2007) argue that these 'unknowledges' are consciously produced and at times this takes the form of those in the centre refusing to allow the marginalized to know" (p.1) Haslanger (2016) calls this 'epistemic objectification' when a group's actual or imagined epistemic weaknesses are wrongly taken to be due to their nature, or essential to them as a group.

In summary, if black children are the recipients of lessons in history, which focus on the narrative of slavery, that negates their progination status, is therefore, fixed in the developing consciousness of the black child, with a subsequent disempowering result. It is noteworthy and relevant, that Ptah and Akhanaten were both regularly excluded from the teaching sessions due to the school's disciplinary regime.

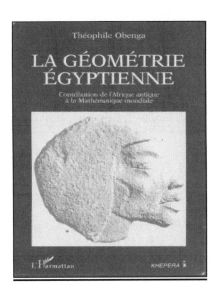

Figure 30 ; head of Akhanaten; Petrie Collection: University College, London, in Obenga 1995- '*The Egyptian Geometry*'

Chapter 8: 'If it doesn't measure up its not Kemetical!: The Black Genesis of Geometry.

In the tomb of Seti II (Userkheperure Meryamun) in the Valley of the Kings (Ta Neset Biti) near Luxor (Waset), carved on the walls are two animals: a celestial crocodile and a horned figure.

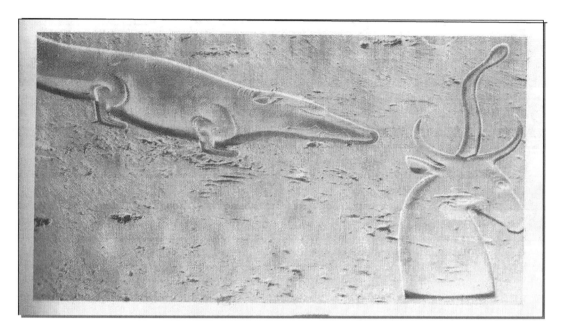

Figure 31: Tomb of Seti I in Temple (2000)

Viewing these animals outside of an Africana worldview may facilitate the reader to miss what is hidden in plain sight. These ancient animals have been geometrically carved with precise accuracy, placement and intent. According to archaeologist and author, Robert Temple (2000), the horned animal is: "Multiply-defined by 26 degree angles: a horizontal line intersecting the tip of the crocodile's snout makes a 26 degree angle with a line which grazes the top of his back [see figure 31]. Whereas a horizontal line intersecting the tip of his forepaw makes a 26 degree angle with a line grazing the bottom of his posterior. Furthermore, a horizontal line intersecting the centre of the horned animal's head makes a 26 degree angle with the tip of the crocodile's back. The crocodile is thus not only zooming down at an angle of 26 degrees, but his actual dimensions are defined by the same angles. We thus find that *the entire composition is governed by a series of golden triangles*. But, there is even more: a horizontal line intersecting the centre of the horned animal's eye forms a 26 degree angle with a line which runs along the edge of the crocodile's own eye; and then goes onto graze the top of the crocodile's back where it meets the other such line. The eyes of the two animals are thus, joined by a golden triangle as well. Their ears are also joined by a further golden triangle: a horizontal line intersecting the tip of the horned animal's ear forms a 26 degree angle with a line to the centre of the crocodile's ear. The tip of the horned animal's central horn is also joined by a golden triangle with the lowest point of the crocodile's body. A horizontal line intersecting the tip of the horn forms an inverted angle of 26 degrees with a line touching the lowest part of the crocodile's body above its forepaw, thus linking the highest point of the horned animal's head with the lowest part of the crocodile's body by an inverted golden triangle.

The use of the golden triangle as the fundamental principle in the canon of Egyptian (Kemite) art, is thus illustrated in massive redundancy. What is even more extraordinary is that this work of art was sealed in a tomb which was never meant to be entered for eternity, so there would be no opportunity for anyone to appreciate all the trouble which was taken over the design" (p.216).

It has been necessary to quote Temple (2000) in its entirety for two reasons: Firstly, in recognition of his acute insight into geometrical representation and the access to his photograph in all of its simplicity and beauty. However, secondly, and perhaps more importantly, Temple's concluding statement ..."the golden triangle… is illustrated in massive redundancy" (ibid) suggests that his Eurocentric paradigm forces him to miss, or rather not understand, the cultural, spiritual and cosmological significance of sacred geometry. Indeed, Kamene (2019) recognizes "in order for us to have a clear understanding of the truest meaning of ancient Kemetic (Egyptian) wisdom, we must think like them, within the context in which they lived, physically, mentally, spiritually and soulfully" (p.2). This tomb carving, deliberately hidden, has more power and significance from an Afrocentric worldview analysis than if it were out in full open display. To delve deeper, Sobek, the crocodile, represents time and blackness: "The constellation Draco was also called the crocodile…the crocodile was a type of sunrise and sunset…an ideograph of blackness" (Straiton, 1927, p.44). Sobek was also associated with fertility and navigation: "One of the tasks of crocodiles with nature is to search for life: they search for water, a crucial element for the fertility of the earth. Like a terrestrial element, they can obtain it in the sources of water, and like a celestial element through rainfall. Therefore, the crocodile is terrestrial, celestial and from the underworld as well" (Pacheco & Ortiz, 2004, p.5). They also live in caves, that have been related to the maternal womb as a passage to, or from the underworld (ibid, p.7); strengthened further, by the feminine essence of the golden triangles which are replete in Seti's (Userkheperure Meryamun) tomb as powerful symbols of creation and duality and therefore, are not "illustrated in massive redundancy" (Temple, 2000, p.216).

"Geometry is defined as knowledge of that which always exists' (Plato VII 375). "The Nile valley, Ethiopia, Nubia and Kemet taught the world, geometry" (Asante, 2020, p.7).
The Egyptians (Kemites) were the first mathematicians. They taught the western world about mathematics. What Pythagoras, Fibonacci, Socrates and other ancient scholars learned, they got from visiting and studying ancient Egypt. To the Egyptians (Kemites), *mathematics was nothing more than an expression of natural rules of the universe"* (Miller 2009, p.9, emphasis added).
As the teaching session transcript below evidences, the 'crocodile' theme is picked up, using the same photograph with each of the teaching groups.(Ptah, Shaka & Menes).

Researcher: (shows the children the picture of animal carving of crocodile & deer from temple of Abydos carved with invisible golden triangles) Now what they did they went down into the temple and carved these animals on a wall this big (points to classroom back wall as scale).

Menes: But why would they do that?

Researcher: Well, they did something very special...

Martin: To remember it

Researcher: Yes, but for a special reason ... why is the crocodile up in the air like that?

Menes: I think the crocodile is trying to pounce on the deer and it is going to block the crocodile like a magnetic field

Researcher: Well, let's ask Ria, because I think she sees something differently

Ria: It might be standing on a rock behind the deer

Researcher: Why are these animals in these positions?

Martin: Well they do like to eat big things

Researcher: I think I'm going to have to show you (takes out picture showing that the animals are geometrically positioned to form intersecting triangles)

Ria, Martin & Menes: TRIANGLES!

Researcher: You see what they did... (Menes interjects)

Menes: I get this now, all the triangles are coming out

Martin: Is that the proper size?

Researcher: No the temple wall is as big as this classroom wall

Martin: WHAT!

Researcher: And so I have reduced this down so that you can make your own triangles... but I can only find 2 and I went from the nose of the crocodile to the horn of the deer, back to the neck and up again (demonstrates an equilateral triangle- using a 12 Kemetic cord)

Researcher: (Demonstrates the errors some children are making. For example, having a piece of cord left over which means that they haven't measured their sides accurately etc - gives out resources, equipment and card for children to experiment)

Menes: Can I get my triangle from my folder that I made from my first day to help me?

Researcher: (Menes requires help with his mapping- so I help him to join the points up) oh no look...

Menes: It's not Kemetical! (uses this word to describe an incomplete triangle)

Researcher: (LAUGHS) What a great new word

Menes: Yes, because it needs to be (demonstrates straightness of cord)

Menes Oh, it's going to fit now...

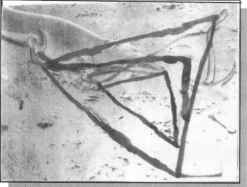

figure 33: 'Menes'

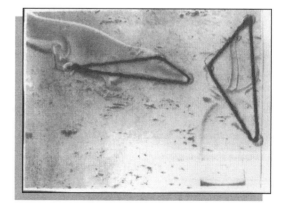

figure 32: 'Ptah'

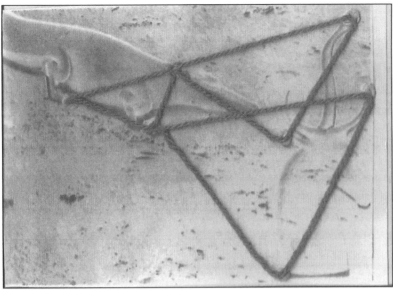
figure 34: 'Shaka'

This short extract, is from a 50 minute, lesson which initially explored language names through etymology and geographical locations. As, a consequence, the exploration of the 'hidden realm' and a deeper probing with the golden triangles was relatively, short in duration. However, the seemingly simple statements made by the children above are in fact, very interesting and innovative in their execution. For example, when asked; *"Why is the crocodile up in the air like that?"* Menes' response: *"I think the crocodile is trying to pounce on the deer and it is going to block the crocodile like a magnetic field"*; suggests that he had retained some of the concepts that we had explored in a previous session on the earth's movements, electric and magnetic field. Here, he is exploring and consolidating, according to King and Swartz (2018): "the conscious recovery of African cosmology" (p.28). This is significant, because the ancient Kemetic netcher Djehuti (know as Thoth/Hermes to the Greeks and Romans: see figure 35) uttered over 5,000 years ago: 'Everything

Figure 35: Djehuti the ntchr of articulate thought, intelligence and wisdom

moves; nothing rests, everything vibrates" (Chandler, 1999, p.79). Here, the depiction of 'movement' 'motion' and 'gesture' in the crocodile image, as a universal principle carved, by the Kemetic mathematician/artist, has arguably been achieved. In keeping with King and Swartz's (2018) reclamation of cultural heritage and the work of Nobles (2017); who stresses the importance of being psychologically freed and intellectually open when one is immersed in the truth of their culture and history. Indeed, the simple yet profound remark made by Menes when attempting to measure one of his hidden triangles exclaimed: *"It's not Kemetical*!"* demonstrates not only the creation of a new adjective from him, which was stimulated by the use of the mathematical equipment of the ancient Kemites; (i.e. he was using the authentic 12 knotted cord). Put simply, for Menes to suffix the noun Kemet to the adjectival *Kemetical* was a natural, lexical utterance. Furthermore, it also suggests that Menes was indeed stimulated, by the earlier aspects of the lesson, in which we discussed the indigenous names of Egypt (Heku ptah- KM, Kham, Kemet).

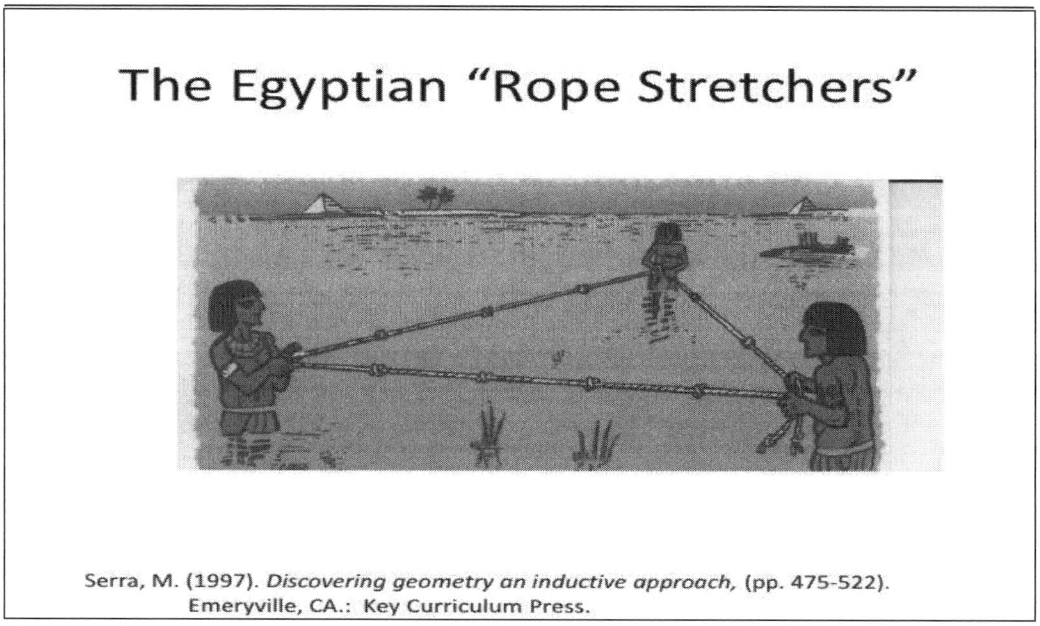

The Egyptian "Rope Stretchers"

Serra, M. (1997). *Discovering geometry an inductive approach,* (pp. 475-522). Emeryville, CA.: Key Curriculum Press.

Figure 36: Kemetic knotted cord

The use of one stimulating image in the teaching sessions of the carved celestial crocodile enabled other groups of children to produce quite different representations of the golden triangle. For example, Ptah (figure 32) chose to use paint to map out his fractal shapes as 'recursive nesting'- as an ever-expanding scene. Ron Eglash (1999) in his seminal text: *African Fractals;* observes: "African architecture tends to be fractal because that is a prominent design in African culture…African creation concepts, are often based on a recursive nesting" (p.39 & p.131). "A design feature "which is not about similarity between right/left or up/down, but rather similarity *between different size frames*" (p.43, original emphasis). Indeed, from a Eurocentric paradigm Eglash (1999) states: "When Europeans first came to Africa, they considered the architecture very disorganized and thus primitive. It never occurred to them that Africans might have been *using a different form of mathematics that they hadn't even discovered yet" (in Koutonin, 2016, p.3, emphasis added).* In contrast, when Shaka (figure 33) chose to depict five scale-expanded triangles, the visual impact of his figure is strongly Ma'atian, particularly through the concept of 'Order and Arrangement', Harmony and Balance (Gadalla, 2001). She (Ma'at) is in essence, cosmic order (Mfundishi, 2016). Gadalla (2000) argues that we must appreciate "their superior cosmic knowledge, for as stated in Asleptus III (25) of Hermetic Texts: …in Egypt all the operations of the powers which rule and work in heaven have been transferred to earth below…it should rather be said that the whole cosmos dwells in (Kemet) as in its sanctuary" (p.10). Shaka's figure is also about the dominance and use of space which is inclusive of both animals, interestingly, Menes' (figure 33) chose to delineate his triangles by mapping them directly onto the animals. In figure 37, [below], from the tip of the crocodile's outer claw, to its eye and from

93

its snout forms an isosceles triangle. Coleman (2018) reminds us that "anything of itself, in itself, times itself is a spiritual w(holistic) and a cosmic natural law. It is noteworthy that land dwelling crocodiles lived 231 million years ago (Reuters, 2015). How did the ancient Kemites conceptualize this knowledge over thousands of years before the famed European scholars such as Plato (approx- 428-348 BCE), Pythagoras (approx 569-475 BCE) and Euclid (approx 325-265 BCE) set foot on the earth? Indeed, Plato himself, writing in his famous text: *Timeaus* (360 BCE), in which he discussed the order and formation of the universe, exposes the Greeks as mere children: "You Greeks are always children; there is no such thing as an old Greek…you are young in soul, every one of you. For therein you possess not one single belief that is ancient and derived from old tradition, nor yet one science that is hoary with age" (22b, in Gutenberg, 2008)

Figure 37: The tip of the crocodile's outer claw, to its eye and from its snout forms an isosceles triangle.

The hidden realm of geometry in the United Kingdom

In 2016, a headline, which caused much controversy, hit mainstream news: "*GCSE pupils to be taught Africans were in Britain before the English*" (Branagan & Craven, 2016). From the outset, this emotive use of polarizing language such as 'Africans' and 'the English' immediately sets up, according to school psychologist and historian Dr Umar Johnson (2015), "the power of subconscious archetypal programming" (lecture presentation). It creates an unconscious set of pictures and locations, which are embedded firmly, in the psyche of the reader's mind as those identities become fixed notions of 'Africans' and 'the English'. In short, our cultural and historical training attaches them as black and white people rigidly situated geographically in Africa and Britain. Many critics such as Sir Roy Strong; V.S. Naipaul; Professor Alan Smithers and Chris McGovern have attacked the course syllabus offered by the Oxford and Cambridge examination Board (OCR). Indeed, Chairman for Real Education, Chris McGovern argues: "The country is being sold down the river by the politically correct brigade and national identity sacrificed for minority groups to feel included" (in Branagan & Craven, 2016, p.3). In a similar vein, Professor Alan Smithers, a specialist adviser to the Commons Education Committee, argues: This seems to be aimed more at indoctrination than education. It is dangerous because a cohesive society depends on an authentic shared view of history" (ibid). In agreement, historian Sir Roy Strong, author of *The Story of Britain* contends:

"The only Africans who came here were a few with the Romans who came and then left! I find it disturbing that *our* children should be taught something that is clearly designed to feed into contemporary problems rather than tell *our* island's story properly" (ibid, p.2, emphasis added). Finally, Nobel literature prize author, V.S. Naipaul claims "This absurd supposition of Africans inhabiting Britain before the English only goes to show how our once esteemed centres of learning…have been insidiously eroded by a dangerous dogma" (ibid). It is interesting to note that Sir Roy Strong's design cover for his book: *The Story of Britain* (1996) is replete with African geometric symbols such as recursive nesting, quincunx fractals and bilateral scaling using the sacred triangle. Would Sir Roy, if made aware of this African genesis to represent his book and his 'island's story' would find this fact more 'disturbing'?

In the Forward to Michael Bradley's *Chosen People from the Caucasus* (1992), professor John Henrik Clarke observes how defenders of the current '*His-story*' curriculum become emotively charged and reactionary when a multidisciplinary, evidenced and historical approach is set in motion: "It opens some long closed historical doors…it disturbs well preserved skeletons and frightens a lot of living people. For the last 500 years, the historical records have been distorted to make people of European descent feel good at the expense of the majority of mankind" (p. i). Indeed, the above critics, in Branagan & Craven (2016), present their arguments without a shred of evidence to substantiate their claims, instead they use language such as: 'dangerous dogma'; 'disturbing'; 'indoctrination'; 'politically correct brigade'; 'absurd'. It appears that to the holders of the status quo, the mere mention of Africans coming first to these lands actually "frightens a lot of living people" (Clarke, p. i, in Bradley, 1992). For example, Sir Roy Strong agues as above that: "The only Africans who came here were a few with the Romans who came and then left!" This episodic and incorrect paradigm fails to acknowledge the written evidence, which indicates what the Roman soldiers observed. This was reported by the Ist century historian Tacitus in his biography: *The Germania and Agricola of Tacitus*. He wrote the following: "Silurum Colorati Vultus - The swarthy complexions of the Silures…Colorati refers to the dark complexion" (Boetticher, 1847, p.157). The second century Roman historian Pliny called them: " Ethiopian indigenes of Britain" (in List, 1999, p.25). Furthermore, the Silures migrated from Spain-the Iberian Peninsula as "there was a mountain in the Spanish Peninsula called Silurus" (Rice-Holmes, 1907, p.399). Similarly, author and historian J. A. Rogers' book: *Nature Knows no Color Line* (1980) …"The Silures, or Western Britons… were very likely of Phoenician or Egyptian descent. Ancient Welsh folk-tales certainly do mention black people, unmistakably Negroes. In the story of Peredur in 'The Mabinogion' the blacks mentioned therein are Silures. Another ancient Welsh poem: Gwadd Luid y Mawr, tells a story of rivalry between black and white - Mawr or Moor" (p.71). In the text: *A new History of Great Britain from the first invasion of it by the Romans under Julius Caesar to the present Time* (1771). Finally, Mourant and Watkin (1952) observe the Irish: '*fear mor*' and Welsh phrases '*gwr mawr*' translated into English as ' great man' (p.33)

"The Silures were the bravest and most organized state in Britain. They were considered one of the bravest of the ancient British nations and defended their country and their liberty against the Romans with the most heroic fortitude" (Henry, 1771, p.179). Indeed, Ivimy (1976) argues that the "Romans pushed the Druids out of England into the Welsh mountains…from father to son in unbroken succession from the time when scientists first came to Wales from Africa three thousand years before" (p.164). Sir Roy Strong and his colleagues present a history devoid of evidence, historical accuracy and calm reasoning. This begs the inevitable question: What would these critical voices make of the physical, cultural, historical and anthropological evidence of the skeleton remains found in Wales over 33,000 years ago; and all over the British Isles, which points to an African origin?

The skeleton, found in Goat's Hole, Paviland, on the Gower Peninsula in Wales, is still referred to as: 'The Red lady'. The bones are in fact those of a man, aged approximately 21 years and dated to 33,000 years old (Bradshaw, 2017, p.1).The burial remains were first discovered in 1823 by Professor of Geology and Dean of Westminster: William Buckland. In his (1823) text, Buckland states a very important cultural phenomenon, which, at the time, perplexed him: "The bones were all stained superficially with a dark-brick red colour, and enveloped by a coating of ruddle (red ochre). Composed of red micaceous oxide of iron, which, stained the earth. And in some parts extended itself to the distance of about half an inch around the surface of the bones" (p.87). The body of the man was also surrounded by netrita littoralis shells and "perforated seashell necklaces identical to *the 75,000 year old shells discovered at the Blombos site in South Africa* (Bradshaw, 2017, p.1, emphasis added). The significance of this cultural burial ritual i.e. the staining of the bones with red ochre and the inclusion of spiral tipped sea shells; is deep with ancient meaning and relevance. Hodgskiss (2015) states: "The use of red ochre dates to the Middle stone age and Middle Paleolithic. The earliest evidence of its use, in Africa dates: **285,000 years**" (p.1). Similarly, "Red ochre symbolizes life blood and life essence: 'blood of earth' or menstrual blood. It has been used in Africa as a ritual substance relating to birth, death and other luminal states" (Graham, 2013, p.32). Therefore, from an Afrocentric paradigm, the Paviland skeleton (figure 39) was ritually prepared and returned to the earth as in the cycle of life.

Figure 39;'The Red lady' of Paviland
(Wikipedia, 2014, credit Ethan Doyle White)

Figure 38 Ochre powder being prepared in Africa

Professor Breuil in 1912, dated the Red lady' to the Aurignacian period (43,000 and 37,000 years) and reported on the Aurignacian painting found in Bacon's Hole, west of the Mumbles, on the coast of Gower. "On entering one of the investigators cried 'Les voila!' and the other 'there they are!" On the right hand wall, at about the level of the eyes, may be seen- not a picture...but a number (ten) horizontal bands, a vivid red, arranged in a vertical series about one yard in height. Similar bands, have been described from the walls of Font de Gaume in Dorgone" (in Bahn & Pettitt, 2009, p. 2). All, dated approximately to the upper Paleolithic age of over 40,000 years old.

We (the authors) stress the importance of avoiding the usual 'media res' research approaches, i.e. starting in the 'middle of things' or using material which ignores earlier evidence of the first inhabitants of the British Isles and Europe. Indeed, many of the research books available are usually 'non-accessible' or 'hidden' from the general public and reveal information, which has always been known amongst the ruling elites.

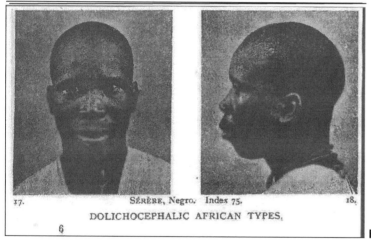

SÉRÈRE, Negro. Index 75.
DOLICHOCEPHALIC AFRICAN TYPES.

Figure 40 (in Ripley,1899, p.44)

"These men, whose remains have been unearthed in caves, and whose implements have been discovered in the river drift of the late glacial epoch, were decidedly dolichocephalic (figure 40). We know that the earliest type of man in Britain was as long headed as the African Negro (Ripley, 1899, p.306). Professor William Boyd Dawkins, an archaeologist and geologist stated; "The Iberians of France and Spain; the Silures of Wales; the Ligures of Southern Gaul and Northern Italy; and the small dark Etruscans, are to be looked upon as ethnological islands isolated by successive invasions. If, we go deep enough, into the past we should find that the whole of Europe was once inhabited by a swarthy non-Aryan population" (1880, p.323). Luke (1990) argues: "The scientific findings of Boule and Vallois (1957); Churchward (1913); Sollas (1911); Diop (1974); Leakey (1980) and others establish the fact that it was indeed a short African race which preceded the taller one; and that this short race was the earliest form of modern man. Going back 100,000 years in Africa and possibly 40,000 in Europe in the form of the Grimaldi man" (p.231). In a previous lecture delivered in the public hall at Manchester in 1879; Professor Dawkins publicly thanked "the labours of Dr Thurnam and Professors Huxley and Busk; Dr Broca in Paris and Professor Virchow in Berlin for their findings" (p.104). On examining "the evidence in this country we find precisely the same class of proof…a small black, long-headed man" (ibid). 'This small, black long-headed man' was, on one hand, recognized for his progeny, however, he was not given, the full status of humanity; for example, author and historian Charles Squire (1910) described the first ancient inhabitant of the British Isles: "it seems to have come originally from some part of either Eastern, Northern, or Central Africa. It spread northward through Europe as far as the Baltic, and Westward, to Spain, France, and our own islands" (pp. 19-20). The 'it' that Squire (1910) described over 100 years ago was given a geographical location by Mackenzie (1917) in his book: *Myths of Crete and Pre-Hellenic Europe*: …"that the description of the bones of an Early Briton of that remote epoch might apply in all essential details to an inhabitant of Somaliland" (p.58). Clearly, these honest historians, were hugely conflicted with their own personal and private positions as these related to the dominance and influence of pseudo scientific racist theories that were so prevalent during this period. However, Professor Boyd Dawkins is quite clear in his understanding and recognition of his own geneology:

"I, for one, being an Englishman, and belonging to the *newest invaders* of this country, look with exceeding reverence upon the *oldest of our population*, and I respect them, not merely as being the oldest, but as being *the introducers of the rudiments of our civilization*" (p.106, emphasis added). This, according to Diop (1974), is a rare moment of historical accuracy because; "Our investigations have convinced us that the West has not been calm enough and objective enough to teach history correctly, without crude falsifications" (p.xiv).

We find the traces of "these lost and overlain races of prehistory as the originators" (Manias, 2012, p.911) of a material culture that is deep in mathematical, geometrical and symbolic meaning. Deep in the ancient history of the Irish countryside; originally named *Ibheriu* the oldest Gaelic name for Ireland; a word that resembles Iberia (Fell, 1989, p.63). There is an age-old site called Dowth (Dubhadh= black). On one of the stones, curiously, no longer available to the public (see figure 40), there is a distinct carved shape that according to Fergusson (1872) "may really be intended to suggest an idea, but of what nature we are not yet in a position to guess" (p.211).

Figure 41: carved shape on stone in Dowth, Ireland (in Fergusson, 1872)

Figure 42: hidden geometry mapped out.

In the methodological application of an Africana lens, we are able to dispense with Fergusson's (1872) 'guesswork' and locate a precise, cultural meaning. Why would the ancients of melanation hide this incredible graphic representation? Because, without 'knowledge of self', it remains hidden and obscure. The sacred triangle is African in its inception. For this reason alone, to decolonize one's perception and schema from a Eurocentric paradigm is both liberating, and informative and very necessary. Indeed, the indigenous people of Ireland came under the title of many appellations: Firbolgs, Tuatha de Danaan, Nemedians, Parthalonians; Fomarians, and Milesians or Giodels as they were all successive black migrations (Ali & Ali, 1992; Fleischler, 2010). Robert List (1999) in his book: *Merlin's Secret. The African presence in the Ancient British Isles* states: "The Irish Tuatha de Danaan, became the dark elves and faeries of a hundred tales told in front of roaring peat fires; the dark, Iberian, non-Aryan Firbolgs of Ireland" (p.25). Squire (1910), reveals the names of these tribes as "*Corca-Oidce*, or 'People of Darkness', *Corca Duibhne* or 'People of the Night' (p.70). The Tuatha de Danaan or 'Danaans' can be traced back to ancient Kemet (Egypt) and in Mediterranean Greece. They were called Melampodes or "'black feet' and in Greek history they were also called 'Danaans' (Whittaker, 2003, p.146). The tribes (tuatha) or the people of Ana/Anu worshipped the goddess Dana, and according to Poe (1997), "the Egyptian word Tanaya is widely understood to refer to the Danaoi, or Danaans, an old name for the Greeks used by Homer" (p.131). Interestingly, in his 8th century poem *Iliad,* the word Danaan and Danaoi appear 138 times (Wikipedia, 2020, p1). In Ireland, as Danu-Ana she led the Irish trinity of Fates and the mountains of Kerry are named after her breasts- The Paps of Anu which can still be viewed today (Graves, 1958, p.409). Finally, in Saxon myth, Danu-Ana became Black Annis in which her benevolent life giving attributes such as the 'Waters of Heaven' and 'Greatest of all Goddesses' was turned into an evil, wicked entity now misinterpreted by an alien patriarchal/masculine culture: "Europeans often visualized demons as black, like Negroes" (Walker,1983, p.221).

In 1963, a plaque unearthed by metal detectors, on the slopes of Cadir Idris near Tal- y- llyn in Wales left many perplexed. Historically, the name Idris is the etymon of Enoch see figure 43 below (Kush, 2000).

Figure 43: Enoch the Ethiopian

He was an Ethiopian priest. This is clearly linked to the sacred knowledge of the Druids which Ivimy (1974) discussed earlier, as those from Africa who the Romans, pushed into the Welsh mountains. The Tal-y-llyn plaque (see figures 44 & 45) is

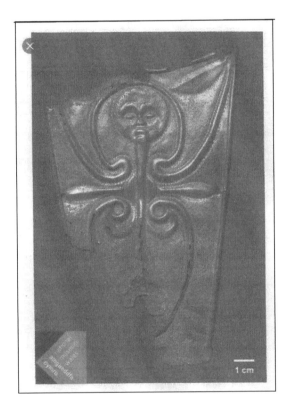

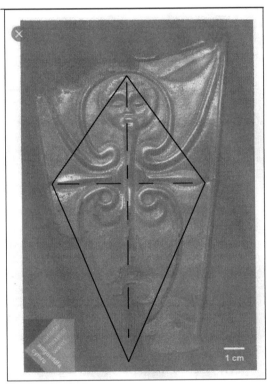

Figure 44: Tal-y-llynn plaque Museum of Wales)

Figure 45: hidden geometry mapped out (Courtesy of

replete with geometry, this masterpiece is a superb example of both skill and cultural will. Figure 44 shows the precise mapping of the two figures (obscured through age), within a quadrant of sacred triangles. Figure 48 forces us to ask the fundamental question: 'Why would the artist create two opposing heads? To locate the answer, we find the ancient African maxim: 'As above so Below' and the concept of "twin-ness, constantly interacting with the Cosmos" (Kamene, 2019, p.49). This duality also signifies the female and male essence of completeness (Marimba, 1994; Finch, 1990;).

Figure 46: photo of Tal-y-llyn in its original state, in Waddell, (2012), p.399.

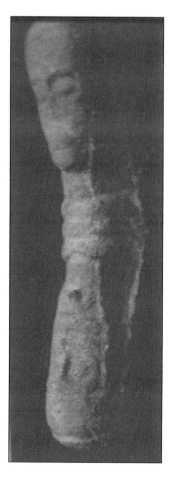

Figure 47: Dogon carving of opposing heads In Laude, (1973), p.72

Figure 48: opposing heads found in Co Clare, Ireland in Sharkey (1975)

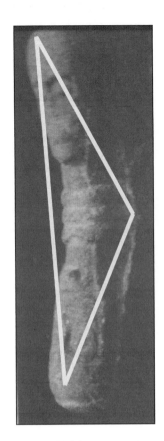

Figure 48: hidden geometry mapped out

Figure 49: hidden geometry
Mapped out

These artifacts (art facts, Kamene, 2019) located in the British Isles, demonstrate that these carriers of a culture where steeped in Ma'atian principles such as Men Nefer which is to be built in perfection. The Universal laws as taught and propagated by the ancient Kemites and ancient Britons, can in fact, be seen through their expressions of art, ritual and thought. Why, for example, do we find a carved Ibis bird in a cave in Derbyshire? Djehuti or later named Thoth by the Greeks and Hermes by the Romans, was the deity of wisdom, articulate speech/thought and writing; also depicted as an Ibis bird. Sacred and divine because of its attributes, the Ibis bird carved in Creswell Crags had been 'Men Nefered', i.e. built in perfection; notably, from its eye to its beak and down to its neck conforms to accurate geometry and has been dated to over 15,000 years old (English Heritage, nd). However, is this, an imprecise carbon dating given by the English Heritage? As their commissioned book: *Britain's Oldest Art: The Ice Age cave art of Creswell Crags* by Bahn & Pettitt (2009), places "the use of the cave probably between 50,000 and 40,000 radio carbon years ago…. and from other sites may have been between 38,000 and 36,000 years ago" (p.25). Clearly, the inhibiting consequences of the Wurm ice ages, need to be taken into account when considering the dating of human occupation. However, Bahn & Pettitt state: "The Interstadial (the warming period) had been preceded by a long period of intense cold when ice sheets in the British Isles reached as far south as the Gower Peninsula of south Wales and north Norfolk, *although they failed to reach Creswell* (p.24, emphasis added). Therefore, why did the English Heritage and the authors (2009) arrive at such an imprecise date for the ibis bird carving? Al-Amin (2013) argues that the "major migrations of Caucasoids into Europe began after 2,000BC when a general expansion out of the Eurasian Great White Forest commenced" (p.238). In Michael Bradley's (1978) text: *The Iceman Inheritance*, he reminds us, that this geographical phenomenon which, according to archaeologist and linguist Gimbutas (1997), signaled the end of 'Old Europe'. Bradley (1978) argues:

"Eurasian Neanderthal-Caucasoids existed from the end of Wurm I, but their population did not reach a level permitting expansion in force until after 1500BC...and the population had not increased sufficiently, so that a 'critical mass' of sorts had been reached" (p.141). The 'Old Europe' which Marija Gimbutas (1997) described was a culture steeped in deep tradition through "their elegant ritual ceramics (the vast majority being female)...long lasting stable societies and the *absence of weapons and organized warfare*" (in Spretnak, 2011, p.2, emphasis added). It is significant that professor Gimbutas recorded the absence of 'weapons and organized warfare' as this clearly suggests that not only did these civilizations co-exist peacefully and culturally, but perhaps more importantly, that they shared a common origin. Indeed, Cultural historian Wayne Chandler (1999) traces this cultural superimposition:

"The Indo-Europeans who went west became the Greeks, Slavs, Germans, Celts, Thracians, Balts, and Illyrians. Those who invaded the eastern areas became the Anatolians, Phrygians, Armenians, Indo-Iranians, and Tocharians...forcing their way into Mesopotamia, Canaan, and finally Northwest India...areas [which] had for millennia been major centers of civilization for people of African descent" (p.117).

In the high northern regions of Scotland, there is a small parish and village called Aberlemno, Forfar, in Angus. The village is notable for its three unique standing carved stones. One of the stones is called the 'Serpent Stone' and is very interesting for its seemingly 'unfinished' appearance; nowhere in the literature (to date) does this 'unfinished' aspect appear as a discussion point or as a simple observation.

Before, commencing with this intriguing aspect of the stone, and in the utilization of an Afrocentric lens, the carved symbols of the dominant images of the snake, 'dumbbell' and mirror take us historically back to Africa and her continent. Indeed, the serpent has been carved so strategically at the top of the stone that this is a major motif of ancient Kemet and has similarly been located in South Africa 75,000 years ago (Athope, 2017). The mirror carved at the bottom right hand corner of the stone is symbolically linked to Akhenaten of the great Third Golden Age (so called 19th dynasty) - the 'Aten' goes back to the old kingdom to denote a circular object such as a mirror (Asante, 2000). According to archaeologist, Catherine Namono (2012), the double circles, placed horizontally in the centre of the stone, are similar to 'dumbbells' that have been found in Uganda, on the ceilings within the Bugiri cave and Dolwe Island. Dr Namono attributes this symbolic artwork to "pygmy groups and their cosmos" (p.404). Why is it that the same symbolic representations can also be found all over ancient Scotland, in places such as Ross-shire, Kirkudbright (Dumfries and Galloway), and the famous Cochno stone found in East Dunbartonshire? The answer lies in the concept of cultural continuity between "people of African descent who almost unilaterally peopled and influenced the world" (Kamene, 2019, p.35). These short, original human beings were respectfully, called: Anu/Twa or Khoi Khoi or Diminutive Black People (DBP), Global Black Diaspora, and the 'seed people' (Churchward, 1913, Dass, 2013-aka Dr Supreme). Accordingly, then, we may ask, what does this information have to do with the carved stone found in Aberlemno? These stones, were carved by a people known as the Picts, who have historically been described as 'a mysterious people' who 'suddenly vanished' and who left no writing or 'images of who they were'[12]. This has become a common narrative in which without thorough interrogation creates: "the general assumption that the Picts were a Caucasian people, which even more modern histories have made no effort to correct" (Al-Amin, 2013, p.22). Indeed, the 1911 Encyclopedia Britannica reported:

"Relics of a pygmy race are supposed to exist now in Sicily and Sardinia, i.e. along the high road between Pleistocene Africa and Europe. Near Schaffhausen (Switzerland), Dr Kollman found skeletal remains of small human beings, which have been regarded by some authorities, as belonging to the European pygmies of the Neolithic period. Some anthropologists of authority believe that a Negroid race at one time existed in northern Europe and may have given rise to the traditional tales of elves, goblins, gnomes and fairies" (p.679).

These 'faeries' or 'little people' were indigenous to Scotland and the regions beyond the highland borders. It is possible to trace the etymon of the word 'fairy' to North Africa and Spain. "Ancient Greek geographers say that the farthest west part of Gaetuli (south of ancient Mauritania & Numidia), is inhabited by the Maurussii and Pharussi (Mauri & Phari). Fari was a name for mining dwarfs, who wash gold and silver sand. The Irish peasants will (sic) speak of 'the good people', 'the gentry' or 'the little people' (Haliburton, 1895, p.8).

---

[12] There is unresolved academic debate as to whether the Book of Kells was authored by the Picts.

Similarly, the word 'dwarf' has the same geographical origin: "There is a town or hamlet in the Sahara, called Adwarfi (a corruption of Alt-Warfi, 'the good people', 'the excellent folk'), and the place is a great centre of the little Adwarfi; in Spain the Nanos[13] are called Adwarfi" (ibid).

In 1892-3, professor Sergi published in the Bulletin of the Royal Medical Academy of Rome an important paper which discussed the African migrations of the Anu, Twa, Khoi Khoi- 'little people' from Africa into the Mediterranean, Europe and as far east as Moscow. His examinations of the skeletons found in Sicily, Italy and in the "Etruscan tombs and near Moscow-all resembling the dwarfs of the Congo" (in Haliburton, p.7). The later Eurasian invasions as noted by Chandler,(1999), Al-Amin, (2013) and Bradley, (1978); support the early research of Scottish physician and lecturer in anthropology and archaeology Robert Munro. In his (1899) text: *Prehistoric Scotland and its place in European Civilization* he states: "The results of my first investigations into the physical characteristics of the earliest races of North Britain appeared to me sufficient to establish the fact that the Aryan nations on their arrival, found the country in occupation of allophylian races ('allos'= other; 'phyla= genesis)", p. 445.

The Picts or 'Pecht' is a word for "dwarf that was used in Scotland...and *Pict-cur* a dwelling place or enclosure of dwarfs is linked to *Pitcur* castle in Forfarshire (currently known as Forfar), Angus in Scotland...the oldest castles in the North Country having been built by dwarf masons" (Haliburton, 1895, p.9). The indigene of this region were known for their incredible knowledge of stonemasonry and metal artistry, i.e. metallurgy and their ability to work with base metals and their transmutations, in particular, the precious sought after metal, gold. "The Picts of Orkney were exceeding pigmies in stature and worked wonderfully in the construction of their cities...but all of them are unquestionably links to one special style of structure of the 'Cyclopean' arch. They are commonly spoken of as beehive houses [figure 51], but their Gaelic name is *bo'h* or *bothan* also *bahun*" (MacRichie, 1893, p.46). From Bantu (Zimbabwe) '*zimba we bahwe*' means houses of stone - '*bahwe* means stone (Etymology Dictionary nd, p.1). This ancient knowledge was in the possession

---

[13] The term Nana is a redublication of the root na. In the Twi language, the root na is defined as that which is rare, precious, ancient, (ancestry), great. The Twi language is derived of our ancestral language of ancient

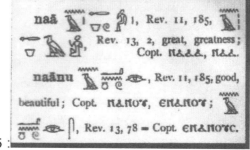

Kamit (Nubia and Egypt) Odwirafo, (2015), p.5 :

of the indigenous DBP and clearly, from an 'outsiders' perspective, must have been viewed as 'magical' and mysterious wizardry.

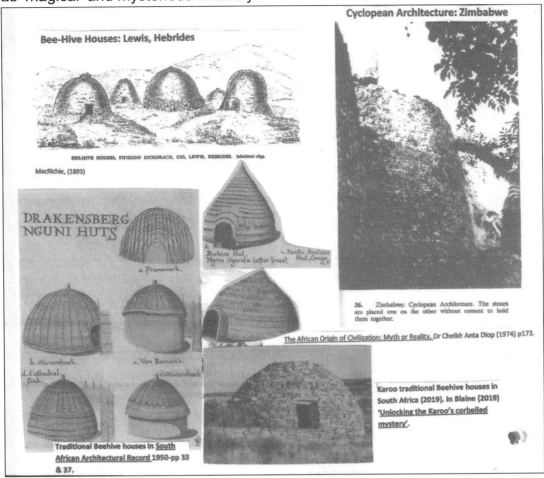

Figure 51: Beehive houses from Africa and Scotland

Within this evidenced paradigm of ancient history and etymology, the beautifully carved stone of Aberlemno is the work and ideation of the 'gentle wee folk' who were masters in stonemasonry and who brought their deep cultural spiritual traditions across the Diaspora. The stone appears 'unfinished' to the observer's eye, however, the mirror provides a vital clue in terms of how to interpret the stone. In placing a wide mirror alongside the edges of the stone, this creates an immediate complete mirror image of the carvings; and when the two sides are joined together this creates

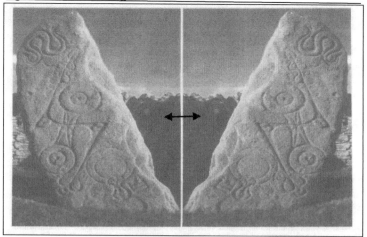

an incredible feat of geometrical precision [figure 53].

Figure 53: representation formed when mirror image of stone is joined together

By joining the two centres of the stone, the Picts created a goddess similar to Tanit who was the "Carthaginian name of the Great Goddess also known as Astarte" (Walker, 1983, p.972), with her triangular 'outer' shape/body - upper and lower, she emerges with circular 'hair-like coils' similar to Hathor - the Great Mother of ancient Kemet. The mirrors are symbolically and traditionally linked to Het Heru/ Hathor in ancient Kemet which historically was known as the ' Hathoric Mirror dance' and is carved in the temple of the sixth dynasty tomb of Mereruka [14] (This dance, according to Morris (2011) "showcased a number of nude

---

[14] Ist Golden Age around 4400-6000 years ago in Mfundishi, 2016, p.28).

performers…[and] possessed a strong solar symbolism" (p.98).The Aberlemno goddess, upon closer inspection has also been carved to depict feminine attributes such as 'breasts' and a 'womb' in her apparent nakedness. Incredible as this discovery is, the next figure demonstrates the African Genesis of Geometry as a cultural phenomenon.

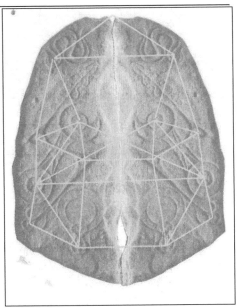

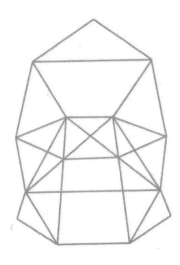

Figure 54: hidden geometry of 'The goddess stone'   **Figure 55: geometrical matrix**

This clear, strategic mapping out of the stones was created by the Picts in their deliberate and meticulous etching of points/dots in the 'dumbbells', mirror handles and lines which depict her upper and lower body. The goddess has been housed within a series of sacred triangles. When the reader looks closely at the triangles around her neck region, there appears to the left and right of her, two pyramidal shapes. This begs the inevitable questions; Why? And then, why would they carve one stone? Asante (2008) argues that not only does a Eurocentric paradigm ignore what is happening from an African perspective, and that a Eurocentric worldview cannot answer the unfolding phenomena because it does not possess the cultural epistemological tools. History tells us that: "The Picts seem to have preserved a tradition that the whole nation was once divided into seven provinces and it would appear that 'the three divisions' over which Dubh, or The Black, held sway, formed that portion of the original seven which remained untouched by whites" (MacRichie,1884, in Rashidi 2011, p.100). However, the Pictish armies, from the Roman invasions in the 1st century to the 14th century (Normans and the Flemings), comprising the Picts, Moors, Gipsies and Faws, would be tested through relentless wars and intrusions on their land and possessions. "The struggle ended in utter discomfiture and the complete downfall of his race (Black Douglases); their estates passing wholly away from them…and bringing about the ruin of the ancient stock… the Red Douglas had put down the Black" (MacRichie, vol 1. p.208). The Pictish or Moorish power had crumbled away, and the latest representatives of

Moorish nobility had sunk into the position of hunted bandits and outlaws" (ibid, pp 14-15).
[15]

The cultural and material evidence of the Aberlemno goddess, gains increasing credibility when one discovers that she is strongly linked "in Scotland to a black goddess anciently known as the 'Nigra Dea' associated with Loch Lorchy and the celebrated Black virgin of Chartes, France, is said to have been brought there from Britain" (Rogers, 1968, p.197). The etymology of *Nigra Dea* from the River Lochy in the great glen of Scotland, can be traced according to King (2003) back to Old Irish (OI) *loch* 'black' with the suffix from the genitive of OI *dia* 'goddess' derived from Old Celtic (OC) deiua – deua – deau – dea, the genitive being OC deiuias – deue – dee – de, thus. Lochdae 'of the black goddess'(p.77). However, King (2003) also suggests that this interpretation is somewhat problematic as there may be a "possible confusion with the near coalescence of the two Old Irish adjectives, *loch*, 'shining' and *lo'ch* 'black' and that both these terms derive from '*louk*' from Proto Indo-European '*leuk*' meaning 'white' or 'shining' (p.77). It is significant that ancient Kemet's 'Hathoric Mirror Dance' as discussed above; has been observed by Mackenzie (1922) in which he connects the two appellations of white and black: "Hathor the cow goddess of Egypt had a black as well as a white form as goddess of the night sky and death. She was the prototype of the black Aphrodite (Venus). In Scotland a black goddess; (the Nigra Dea in Adamnan's Life of Columba), was associated with Loch Lochy" (p.164). Indeed, a Pictish tribe mentioned by Ptolemy links this very point; " *Logi* which is commonly thought to be cognate with OI Loch, and to mean 'The Black Ones, possibly 'The Ravens' further illustrates this point " (Ahlqvist, 1975, in King, 2003, p.87). The very fact that the Nigra Dea goddess was located literally and symbolically with water and situated by the River Lochy is highly significant from an African paradigm. Indeed, the sacred primordial waters of Nun with her powerful feminine attributes were highly revered throughout Kemet in the mother continent (Nobles, 2017; Barashango, 1991; Kamene, 2019; Imhotep, 2011). If one considers this synthesis with Scottish hydronymy (i.e. the study of names of bodies of water and the origins of those names through history), then, the adjectives as proposed by King (2003) such as ''shining' and 'reflective black' gain ascendency in the visual power of the Aberlemno goddess. She has a bright striking luminescence that appears to radiate out from the stone, which the Pictish artist so cleverly captured. Therefore, in light of this evidence, it would seem most appropriate to name her *'The Shining Black Goddess'*.

This loss of culture, tradition and way of life, inevitably gave way, according to Chandler (1999) to a "diametrically opposed mindset to the philosophical mores of the invaded Afro-Asiatic civilizations with their resultant destructive ideologies" (p.118). One of those

---

[15] McRitchie gives the names of several of these Negro families whose names are famous in English history and American history too. One of these is the celebrated Douglas, one of the ancestors of the present royal family of Britain: in Gaelic language –'Sholto-du-glash- 'behold the black or swarthy-coloured man' from which he obtained the name Sholto the Douglas" Rogers, (1968), p.198.

destructive ideologies was "the subjugation, disdain, inferiority, and impurity of women" (ibid). Indeed, Al-Amin (2013) argues: as newer invaders rose to power over the centuries - masculine gods became ever more dominant, subjugating the Feminine Principle or Great Mother concept nearly everywhere, over time" (p.113). This factor may answer, in part, why the Picts chose to 'hide' the great goddess in their stone carving in Aberlemno. However, the stone is also a demonstration of the 'magic' and power of the 'seed people' as great mathematicians; and by engaging within an Afrocentric paradigm, this enables the necessary action of decolonizing the curriculum to liberate the minds of our children. More than ever, the time is now to rescue and reclaim our material culture.

Chapter 9: Conclusion

The central philosophical and pedagogical tenet shared by the authors in the research theory, fieldwork and evidence analysis that has produced this book is that engaging within an Afrocentric paradigm, enables the necessary action of decolonizing the curriculum to liberate the minds of our children.

This research has become even more prescient and imperative within the context of the global awakening to the fact that 'Black Lives Matter'. The continuing systemic oppression of Black communities at the end of the second decade of the twenty first century, culminating in the escalation of murders of black civilians by police in the USA, has finally sparked a global movement.

For too long, researchers and concerned organisations have concentrated on appointing commissions, subsequent data collection and the submission of reports to national governments and police commissioners. However well evidenced those reports have been, the majority have been allowed, after brief initial 'soundbites', to languish, unactioned. Therefore, minimal empowerment for the Black community has resulted from this plethora of Acts and Reports.

Our aim, and the main focus of this research-based book, is on education and improving the schooling experiences of Black individuals. There is currently much debate about 'decolonising the curriculum'. To the authors, this is crucial, as the fieldwork described and analysed in this book has evidenced that if children [learners] recognise themselves in the taught curriculum themes, they will become more involved, self-motivated and effective as learners. "White students are educated to be rulers and makers of this society. Black students are taught to synthesise the experiences and memorize the conclusions of another people. The consequence of such education is that many blacks, if not most, are inclined to confuse their interests with oppressive structures. Black studies programmes must develop black youth with a revolutionary style of identity.' [Turner, 1971 pp. 12-17].

This book, attuned to the global protests, is an attempt to support the actualization of Turner's vision of Black agency and empowerment. If we are truly serious in our endeavours Paget Henry (2006) demands that "a clearing of the way" must ensue. This "clearing of the way" is necessary to decolonize the curriculum and to 'pull apart' European colonialism to "prepare the ground for such new phenomenological possibilities" (p.2). The time is here and now to teach our children the hidden histories, the stolen histories, and the forgotten histories of global majority people.

Available Resources: Example of Purple Unit-'People and Places'

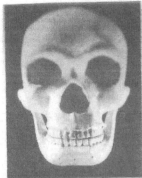

"A gravel pit in the English village of Swanscombe not far from London has yielded important fossil clues. The Thames Valley site is a well-known collector's paradise, possibly a place where hunters camped to kill big game coming to drink from the river. In June 1935, when local cement workers noticed a piece of bone protruding from the gravel bank turned out to be part of a skull of 'prehistoric' man who had died in his early twenties. Geological studies show that the laying down of the gravels which contained the Swanscombe remains, were preceded by two major glaciations and an intervening warmer interglacial stage. The first glaciations saw the migration of hunters out of Africa, as indicated by findings at the Esacale and Vallonet caves in France. Then after the ice retreated in the interglacial stage, there was another glaciation. The Torralba-Ambrona sites belong to this period. Swanscombe man lived during the latter part of the subsequent interglacial stage, about **250,000 years ago**, in a most comfortable climate. In fact, as far as the weather is concerned, that was the time to be in England as elephants and rhinoceroses which had come from Africa over the Dardanelles land bridge browsed in warm Thames valley forests.

In 1933 another fossil skull was found in a gravel pit near the village of Steinheim in western Germany; and may have something to tell us about Swanscombe man (both skulls were found in interglacial deposits) **and members of the same species. Swanscombe man like Steinheim man are both definitely Homo sapiens**" (p.152-155).

The Emergence of Man, John E. Pfeiffer (1969)

Stages in reconstruction of Steinheim man, one version of early *Homo sapiens*, front view: (top) skull in plaster; (center) building up muscles and skin with clay; (bottom) completed bust (*Courtesy of Wanda Steslicka-Mydlarska, Polish Academy of Sciences*)

Homo sapien: Swanscombe skull discovered in Kent, Great Britain. - Image ID: WHA342

https://www.alamy.com/homo-sapien-swanscombe-skull

The Zambian government is still pursuing a claim, first made in 1972, for the return of this famed Rhodesian Man from the Natural History Museum in London.

However, the UK government has refused to release key documents relating to the case, according to the Art Newspaper.

The 250,000-year-old fossilised skull was discovered in a mine in what was then Northern Rhodesia in 1921. The skull represents a Homo species that lacks some of the characteristics of extinct Neanderthals and modern mankind.

Rhodesian Man (Homo rhodesiensis) provides further evidence that humans came out of Africa. Instead of linear evolution—one species replacing the previous one—Africa was probably a melting pot of interbreeding human species, where Rhodesian Man may have lived alongside early Homo sapiens.

After the skull was discovered, the Rhodesia Broken Hill Development Company, which owned the mine, donated it to the Natural History Museum. It is one of the museum's greatest treasures, representing invaluable evidence about human evolution.

In July 2019 The Art Newspaper submitted a request to the National Archives for three papers relating to discussions on the return of Rhodesian Man, removed from a 1973 file, to be opened up under the Freedom of Information Act. It seems surprising that 47-year-old papers relating to the 1921 discovery of a 250,000-year-old skull should be quite so sensitive.

These three pages took officials nearly six months to review, but the Foreign and Commonwealth Office finally refused to release the papers in February, concluding that it "would harm UK relations with Zambia" and "would be detrimental to the operation of government and not in the UK's interest".

Extensive Foreign and Commonwealth Office files provide an insight into what has gone on behind the scenes over the original claim. In 1972 the Zambian foreign ministry wrote to the UK high commission in Lusaka, arguing that the skull was "vital to the history of Zambia" and its return was requested.

The UK's main argument against the claim was that the museum was legally unable to deaccession. Under a 1963 law, the museum can only deaccession duplicates, items unfit for use or post-1850 printed material. It also said the skull is normally on display and accessible for serious scientific research.

The fossilised skull of Rhodesian Man and other bones were discovered in 1921, 90 feet beneath the surface in the Broken Hill lead and zinc mine in what was then Northern Rhodesia. They were found by a Swiss supervisor, Tom Zwigelaar, and an unnamed African miner. Zwigelaar initially displayed the skull on a pole, to frighten his African miners, before it was spotted by a doctor who realised its potential significance.

https://www.facebook.com/Untold-Wisdom-Knowledge-of-Ta-Neter

Zambia

Kent

References

Ackah. W. (2014) **"Why isn't my Professor Black**? www.dtmh.ucl.ac.uk

Ackah, W. (2014) **British Universities need Black Studies**. The Guardian. Wednesday, 14 th May http://www.theguardian.com/commentisfree/2014/may/14/british-universities-need-black-studies

Adams. R (1993) **African-American Studies and the State of the Art. Africana Studies: A Survey of Africa and the African Diaspora.** (ed) Azeveto. M. Carolina Academic Press, pp. 25- 45

African Creation Energy (2010) **The Sciences of Sciences and the Science in Sciences. The Scientific and Mathematic Method in Ancient and Traditional African Culture and Philosophy.** Version 1.0- USA

Akbar. N. (1984) **Africentric social sciences for human liberation**. Journal of Black Studies, 14 (4), pp. 395-414

Akoto. K.A. & Akoto. A.N. (1999) **The Sankofa Movement**. Okoyo Infocom; Washington DC: USA

Akua. C. (2012) Education for Transformation. The keys to releasing the genius of African American students. Imani Enterprises-Teacher Transformation Institute, Atlanta USA.

Akua C. (2019) **Introducing Dr Chike Akua with Professor Kaba Hiawatha Kamene** http://www.youtube.com

Al- Amin. N. (2013) True Myth: Black Vikings of the Middle Ages. Trafford Publishing, USA & Canada.

Allal. L. & Ducrey G.P. (2000) **Assessment of-or in-the zone of proximal development.** Learning & Instruction 10: pp. 137-152

Alexander. A.B.D. (1907) **A Short History of Philosophy**. James Maclehose & Sons: Glasgow.

Alexander. R.J. (2005) **Culture, dialogue and learning: Notes on an emerging pedagogy.** Paper presented at the International Association for Cognitive Education and psychology conference, July Durham UK.

Ali. A. & I. Ali. (1992) **The Black Celts: An ancient African civilization in Ireland and Britain**. Punite Publications, Caerdydd: Cymru

Alkalimat. A. H I. & McWorter. G (1969) **The Ideology of Black Social Science**. The Black Scholar, vol 1 (2), December, pp. 28-35

Allal. L. & Ducrey G.P. (2000) Assessment **of-or in-the zone of proximal development.** Learning & Instruction 10: pp. 137-152

Ani, M. (1994) **Yurugu: An African Centred Critique of European Cultural Thought and Behavior.** African World Press, New Jersey: USA

Al-Saji. A. (2014) **A Phenomenology of Hesitation: Interrupting Racializing Habits of Seeing**. In (ed) Emily Lee: Living Alterities. Phenomenology, Embodiment and Race. State University of New York Press, Albany, USA.

Apple, M. (2001) "**Education and Curricular Restructuring and the Neo-liberal and Neo-conservative Agendas: Interview with Michael Apple**" Curriculo sem Fronteriras, vol 1 (1): 1-xxvi, Jan/June.

Appiah. K.A. (2010) Europe **upside down: Fallacies of the New Afrocentrism**. In R. R. Grinker; S.C. Lubkemain & C. B. Stener: Perspectives on Africa. A reader in culture, history and representation. Wiley-Blackwell Publication

Archer. L (2008) **The Impossibility of Minority Ethnic Educational 'Success'? An Examination of the Discourses of Teachers and Pupils in British Secondary Schools**. European Educational Research Journal. Vol 7 (1) pp. 89-106.

Asante. K.M. (1988) **Afrocentricity**. Africa World Press, Trenton, NJ, USA.

Asante. K. M. (1990) Kemet, **Afrocenticity and Knowledge**. Africa World Press; Trenton, NJ: USA

Asante. K.M. (1998) **The Afrocentric Idea**. Temple University Press, Philadelphia, USA. African American Publishing: USA

Asante. K.M. (2000) **The Egyptian Philosophers:** African American Publishing: USA

Asante. K.M. & Mazama. A. (2002) Egypt **Vs Greece and the American Academy. The debate over the birth of civilization.** African American Images: Chicago, Illinois USA.

Asante. K.M. (2003) Afrocentricity **and the Eurocentric Hegemony of Knowledge: Contradictions of Place. Critical Theory: Diverse Objects, Diverse Subjects**, Volume 22, pp. 61-70.

Asante. M. K. (2004) **An African Origin of Philosophy: Myth or Reality?** http://www.asante.net

Asante. K.M. (2007) **An Afrocentric Manifesto**. Polity Press, Cambridge. UK.

Asante. K.M (2009) **A Quick Reading of Rhetorical Jingoism: Anthony Appiah and his Fallacies.** http://www.asante.net

Asante. K. M. (2011) **De-Westernizing Communication: Strategies for Neutralizing Cultural Myths**. http://www.asante.net

Asante. K.M. (2014) **An African Origin of Philosophy: Myth or Reality?** http://dyabukam.com

Asante. K. M. (2017) **CFA Strategies for empowering the next generation**. http://www.youtube.com

Asante. K.M (2018) **Afrocentricity: Keynote speaker Dr Asante** at the Michael J. Grant campus on February 15th, Brentwood: New York USA.

Asante. K.M. (2020) I AM Afrocentric and Pan-African: A Response to Tawanda Sydesky Nyawasha on Scholarship in South Africa. Journal of Black Studies, January 30th: http://doi.org/10.1177/0021934720901602

Athope. D. (2017) Stone Snake of South Africa: First human worship 70,000 years ago. March 5th https://damienmarieathope.com

Ausburn. L. & Ausburn. F. (1978b) **Visual Literacy: background, theory and practice**, PLET 15 (4) pp. 291- 297.

Bahn. P. & Pettitt. P. (2009) **Britain's Oldest Art. The Ice Age cave art of Creswell Crags.** English Heritage, Swindon, UK.

Banks. W.C. (1992) **The Theoretical and Methodological Crisis of the Afrocentric Concept**. Journal of Negro Education, 61 (3), pp. 262-272.

Bacon. F. (1620) **Novum Organum, Book 1, Aphorism**. Translation by J. Spedding, R. L. Ellis & D.D. Heath (1863) Taggard and Thompson Publishers, Boston, USA.

Barashango. I. (1989) **Afrikan Woman the Guardian Angel.** IVth Dynasty Publishing Company, Washington DC

Barashango. I. (1991) **Afrikan Genesis: Amazing Stories of Man's Beginnings**. Afrikan World Books, Baltimore MD 21217.

Barashango. I (2017) **A Message to the People**. http://www.youtube.com

Barthes, R. (1977) **Image-Music-Text**. London: Fontana

Bauval.R. & Brophy. T. (2013) Imhotep the African: Architect of the Cosmos. Disinformation Company LTD.

Bernal. M. (1987) **Black Athena: The Afroasiatic roots of classical civilization (volume 1). The fabrication of ancient Greece 1785-1985.** Rutgers University Press

Bernier. F. (1684) **Nouvelle Division De La Terre. Par les differentes especes ou races d'homme qui l'habitent.** Journal Des Scavans, April, pp.133-140

Bigford, W. (2013) Academic **success, resilience and ways of being among high achieving African – Caribbean pupils.** School of Education. The University of Birmingham.

Blaine. S. (2019) Unlocking the Karoo's Corbelled Mystery. September 27th; http://www.experiencenortherncape.com

Bloor. D. (1976) **Knowledge and social imagery.** Routledge and Kegan Paul, Henley.

Boetticher. W (1847) **The Germania and Agricola of Tacitus.** Harper & Brothers Publishers, New York: USA.

Bogoshi. J. Naidoo. K. & Webb. J. (1987) **The Oldest Mathematical Artefact.** The Mathematical Gazette, vol 71 (458), p.294.

Bond. H.M. (1934) **The education of the Negro in the American social order.** New York, NY: Octagon Books.

Bond. H.M. (1935) **The curriculum and the Negro child.** The Journal of Negro Education, 4 (2), pp.159-168.

Bonilla-Silva, E. (2010) **Racism Without Racists: Color-Blind Racism and Racial Inequality in Contemporary America.** Lanham, MD: Rowman & Littlefield.

Boser, U. Wilhelm, M. Hanna, R. (2014) **The Power of the Pygmalion Effect: Teacher Expectations Strongly Predict College Completion.** Center for American Progress, October 6th
Boule. M & Vallois. H. (1957) **Fossil Men: A Textbook of Human Paleontology.** Thames & Hudson Publishers.

Bourdieu. P. (1977) **Outline of a Theory.** Cambridge: Cambridge University Press.

Bourdieu, P. (1986/2011) **The forms of capital.** In A.R. Sadovnik (Ed), Sociology of education: A critical reader (2nd Ed, pp. 83-96. New York, NY: Rutledge.

Bowles. S. & Gintis. H. (1976) **Schooling in Capitalist America. Educational Reform and the Contradictions of Economic Life.** Harper Collins: Canada

Boyle. B. & Charles. M. (2008) **Are we doing it right? A review of the assessment for learning strategy.** Primary Leadership Today Vol 2 issue 14 p.20-24

Boyle. B & Charles. M. (2010) **Tightening the Shackles: The Continued Invisibility of Liverpool's British African Caribbean Teachers.** Journal of Black Studies, vol 42 (3), pp 427-435

Boyle. B. & Charles. M. (2013) **Formative assessment for Teaching & Learning** SAGE

Boyle. B. & Charles. M. (2016) **How can only 18 black teachers working in Liverpool represent a diverse teaching workforce? A critical narrative**. Journal of Inclusive Education; vol 20, (8) pp. 871-888

Bradley. M. (1978) **The Iceman Inheritance**. Warner Books, New York: USA.

Bradley. M. (1992) **Chosen People from the Caucasus**. Third World Press, Chicago: USA

Branagan. M. & Craven. N. (2016) **GCSE pupils taught Africans were in Britain before the English**, 9th January http://www.dailymail.co.uk

Bradshaw (2017) The Red Lady. http://www.bradshawfoundation.com

Brittain, E. (1976) **Multiracial Education: Teacher Opinion on Aspects of School Life**. Educational Research, vol 18, (3) pp.182-191

Browder. A. (1992) **Nile Valley Contributions to Civilizations**. Institute of Karmic Guidance. Washington DC, USA.

Brown. S. (2016) **Discourse on Africana Studies: James Turner and Paradigms of Knowledge.** Diasporic Africa Press Inc, New York.

Buchanan. P.J. (2002) **The Death of the West. How Dying Populations and Immigrant Invasions Imperil our Country and Civilization.** Thomas Dunne Books

Budge. W. (1907) **The Egyptian Sudan**, vols I & II. London: Kegan, Trench & Co.

Bullington. J. (2013) **The Expression of the Psychosomatic Body from a Phenomenological Perspective.** Vol III, Springer Briefs in Philosophy, New York & London.

Burgess. S. (2016) "**Will Britain ever have a Black Prime Minister**? BBC News. http://www.youtube.com

Burrell, T (2010) **Brainwashed. Challenging the Myth of Black Inferiority**. SmileyBooks, Hay House, Inc

Butler. J. (1993) **Endangered/Endangering: Schematic Racism and White Paranoia** in (ed) Goodwin-Williams. R.   Reading Rodney King, Reading Urban Uprising. New York, Routledge, USA.

Bynum. E.B. (2012) **Dark Light Consciousness: Melanin, Serpent Power and the Luminous Matrix of Reality.** Inner Traditions, Vermont, USA

Carroll. K.K. (2008) **African Studies and Research Methodology: Revisiting the Centrality of the Afrikan** Worldview. Journal of Pan African Studies, vol, 2 (2), March, pp. 4-27

Carruthers. J. (1999) **Intellectual Warfare**. Third World Press. Chicago, USA

Chandler. W. B. (1999) Ancient Future. The Teachings and Prophetic Wisdom of the Seven Hermetic Laws of Ancient Egypt. Black Classic Press, USA.

Chandler. D. (2002) **Semiotics: The Basics**. Routledge, London UK

Chan. Z.C.Y. Fung. Y.L. Chien. W.T (2013) **Bracketing in Phenomenology: Only Undertaken in the Data Collection and Analysis Process.** The Qualitative Report, vol 18 (59), pp. 1-9.

Charles. M. & Boyle. B. (2014) **Using Multiliteracies & Multimodalities to Support Young Children's Learning** SAGE
Charles. M. (2017) **18 Black teachers in Liverpool, January 2017 no change?** OBV - Operation Black Vote http://www.obv.org.uk

Charles. M. (2019) **Everyone Matters: Damaged histories, the UK schooling system & the myth of Black African Caribbean inferiority**. Unpublished PhD thesis: Leeds University

Churchward. A. (1913) **The Signs and Symbols of Primordial Man**. George Allen & Company LTD, New York: USA

Clark. S. P. (1964) **Literacy for liberation**. Freedom ways, Ist Quarter, New York: Freedom ways Associates.

Clarke. J.H. (1986) African **Contributions to Mathematics, Science, and Technology.** In Teaching Mathematics, volume I: Culture, Motivation, History, and Classroom Management. (ed) Oswald .M.T. Ratteray. Institute for Independent Education Inc, Washington D.C. USA

Clarke. J.H. (1993) African **People in World History**. Black Classic Press; Baltimore, USA

Coard. B. (1971) **How the West Indian Child is made Educationally Sub-normal in the British School System.** New Beacon.

Coard. B. (2005) **Why I wrote the ESN book**. The Guardian Saturday 5th February http://www.theguardian.com/education/2005/feb/05schools.uk

Cobb. C. (2011) Freedom's **struggle and Freedom schools**. Monthly Review, 63 (3) July-August, pp. 1-11.

Coleman. B.T. (1991**) Ma'at: The essence of Truth, Justice, Balance and the African Wa**y. Panther Prince Publications, New York, USA

Coleman. B.T. (2018) **Booker T. Coleman: Black people still don't get it, part 7** http://www.youtube.com

Collins National Dictionary (1972) By Collins London and Glasgow.

Collins. P.H. (1991) **Black Feminist Thought**. Routledge: New York & London.

Cooper. A.J. (1892/1969) **A voice from the South by a black woman of the South**. New York: Negro Universities Press

Croach. S. (1995-1996) **The Afrocentric Hustle**. The Journal of Blacks in Higher Education, no 10, winter, pp. 77-82.

Crummel. A. (1898) **Attitude to the American mind toward the Negro intellect. Occasional Papers,** American Negro Academy, (3), pp. 8-19.

Curry. T. (2017) **The Man-Not. Race, Class, Genre, and the Dilemmas of Black Manhood**. Temple University Press, Philadelphia, USA

Dames. M. (1976) **The Silbury Treasure: The Great Goddess**. Thames & Hudson, UK.

Dass. S. aka Dr Supreme (2013) **When the World was Black. The Untold History of the Worlds' First Civilizations.** Supreme Design Publishing, Atlanta: USA.

Dawkins. W.D. (1879) **Our earliest Ancestors in Britain**. A lecture delivered in the Public Hall, Collyhurst, Manchester; January, 18[th.]

Dawkins. W.D. (1880) **Early Man in Britain and his place in the Tertiary Period.**

Department of Education and Science (1981) **West Indian Children in our schools: Interim report of the committee of inquiry into the education of children of from ethnic minority groups** (The Rampton Report). London HMSO.

Department of Education & Science [1985] Better Schools: A Summary. Department of Education & Science/Welsh Office, March 1985. London: HMSO.

Department for Education (2014) Promoting **fundamental British values as part of SMSC in schools. Departmental advice for maintained schools.** November.

Department for Education (2015) **Early years foundation stage profile results in England, 2014/15**. October 2015.

Department for Education (2017a) **Schools, pupils and their characteristics: January 2017**. (June 2017).

Department for Education [2018] Gov.UK. Ethnicity Facts & figures. https://www.ethnicity-facts-figures.service.gov.uk

Desmond. M. Emirbayer. M. (2009) "**What is racial domination?**" DuBois Review 6

(2), pp.335-355.

Dewey. J. (1902) **The Child and the Curriculum**. The University of Chicago Press.

Diop, C.A. (1974,1989) **The African Origin of Civilization. Myth or Reality**. Lawrence Hill Books.

Diop. C.A. (1981) **Civilization or Barbarism: An Authentic Anthropology**. Lawrence Hill Books.

Dixon. R.B. (1923) **The Racial History of Man**. Charles Scribner's Sons: New York,

Dixon. V. (1971) **An Alternative America. Beyond Black or White**. Little Brown and Company, Boston USA.

Dixon. V. (1976) **Worldviews and Research Methodology. In African Philosophy Assumptions and Paradigms for Research on Black Persons**. (eds) King.L; Dixon. V. & Nobles. W. Fanon Center, Los Angeles: USA.

Drew. A. Sleek. S & Mikulak. A. (2016) When the Majority becomes the Minority. Association for Psychological Science. April: http://www.psychologicalscience.org

Du Bois. W.E.B. (1898b) **The Study of the Negro Problems**. The Annals of the American Academy of Political and Social Science, (Jan) pp.1-23.

Du Bois. W.E.B. (1903) **The Philadelphia Negro. A Social Study.** Schocken Books, New York USA.

Du Bois. W.E.B. (1903/1965) **The souls of Black Folk. In Three Negro Classics** (ed) Franklin. J.H. Avon Books; Harper Collins Publishers, New York: USA.

Du Bois. W.E.B. (1920) **On Being Black**. New Republic (21), pp. 338-341.

Du Bois. W.E.B. (1935/1972) **Black Reconstruction in America**. New York, NY: Atheneum.

Dweck. C. (2006) **Mindset: How you can fulfil your potential**. Ballantine Books.

Dyer, R. (1988) **White Screen**, volume 29 (4) 1st October, pp. 44-65.

Easton. M.G. (1897) **Easton's Illustrated Bible Dictionary**. Third edition published by Thomas Nelson.

Encyclopedia Britannica (1911)

Edwards, B. (2017) **NJ Elementary school faces backlash over slave-auction poster assignment**, 13th March; http://www.theroot.com

Edwards, J. (2017) **Rochester Grammar School criticised for year 8 slavery worksheet.** 12th July http://www.kentonline.co.uk

Eglash. R. (1999) **African Fractals. Modern Computing and Indigenous Design**. Third Paperback Printing, USA.

Ellison, K. (2015**) Being Honest about the Pygmalion Effect**. 29th October http://discovermagazine.com/2015/dec/14-great-expectations

Ellse, M. (2016) **If we are all racists, why do black African kids outperform whites?** http://www.conservativewoman.co.uk

English Heritage (nd) **Prehistory: Art.** http://www.english-heritage.org.uk

Encyclopaedia Britannica (1911), volume 22, p.679.

Emdin. C. (2016) **For White folks who teach in the hood...and the rest of y'all too**: **Reality Pedagogy and Urban Education**. Beacon Press Publishers.

Etymology Dictionary (nd) http://www.etymonline.com

Fanon F. (1967) The Wretched of the Earth Trans. Constance Farrington (Harmondsworth, UK: Penguin)

Fanon. F. (1967) **Black Skins, White Masks**. Grove Press: New York, USA.

Fanon. F. (1965) **A dying colonialism**. New York: Grove Press, USA.

Fell. B (1989) **America B.C. Ancient Settlers in the New World**. Pocket Books New York, USA.

Ferguson. A. (2000) Bad **boys: Public schools in the making of Black masculinity**. Anne Arbor University of Michigan Press.

Ferguson. H.E. (2014) **Why the term 'Minority' is problematic**. http://blackyouthproject.com/why-the-term-minority-is-problematic

Fergusson. J. (1872) Rude **Stone Monuments in all Countries: Their Age and Uses**. John Murray Publishers, London: UK.

Finch. C. S. (1990) **The African Background to Medical Science**. Karnak House, London: UK.

Finch. C.S. (1996) **Still Out Of Africa**. http://www.melanet.com/clegg_series/maat0497.html

Flemming. T. K. (2017) Africology: **An Introductory Descriptive Review of Disciplinary Ancestry**. Africology: The Journal of Pan African Studies, Vol 11, (1), December, pp. 319-386.

Fontaine. W.T. (1940) **An interpretation of contemporary Negro thought from the standpoint of the sociology of knowledge**. Journal of Nero History, 25 (1), pp. 6-13.

Foss. K.A. & Foss. S. K. (1994) **Personal Experience as Evidence in Feminist Scholarship**. Western Journal of Communication, 58 pp. 39-43.

Freire, P. (1970) **Pedagogy of the Oppressed**. New York: Herder & Herder.

Freire, P. (1976) **Education: The Practice of Freedom**. Writers and Readers Publishing Cooperative; London.

Fu-Kiau. K.K.B. (2001) African **cosmology of the Bantu-Kongo, tying the spiritual knot: Principles of life and giving**. New York: Athelia Henrietta Press.

Gadalla. M. (2000) Egyptian **Harmony. The Visual Music.** Tehuti Research Foundation, Greensboro, NC, USA.

Gadall. M. (2001) **Egyptian Divinities. The All who are THE ONE**. Tehuti Reserach Foundation, Greensboro, NC, USA.

Gadalla. M. (2016) **The Ancient Egyptian Metaphysical Architecture**. Tehuti Research Foundation. Greensboro, NC, USA.

Gergen. K.J. (2002**). Psychological science in a postmodern context**. American Psychologist, 56, pp. 803-813.

Gearing. R.E. (2004) Bracketing **in research: A Typology**. Qualitative Health Research, 14, pp.1429-1452.

Gallagher. J. (2018**) Remarkable decline in fertility rates**. http://www.bbc.co.uk. 9th November.

Gaillard. J. & Reid, R. (2014) **Challenges to Analysis of Ancestral Inference Using Mitochondrial DNA Hyper-variable Region 1 SNP Typing**. International Journal of Health Sciences, June, Vol 2 (2) pp.1-15.

Garnet. H.H. (1843/1972) **Address to the slaves of the United States of America**. In S.Stuckey (ed), *The ideological origins of Black nationalism* (pp. 168-170). Beacon Press: Boston, USA.

Gibbons. A. (2009) **Africans' Deep Genetic Roots Reveal their Evolutionary Story**. Science. Vol 334, Ist May 2009 p.575.

Gillborn. D. (2002**) Education and institutional racism**. Institute of Education, University of London.

Gillborn. D. (2008) **Racism and Education: Coincidence or Conspiracy?** London: Routledge.

Gilliam, W.S. Maupin, A. Reyes, C. Accavitti, M. Shic, F. (2016) **Do Early Educators' Implicit Biases Regarding Sex and Race Relate to Behaviour Expectations and Recommendations of Preschool Expulsions and suspensions**. Yale University Child study Centre, September 28th.

Goff. P.A. Jackson, M.C. Di Leone. B. Culotta. C.A. DiTomasso. N.A. (2014) **The Essence of Innocence: Consequences of De-humanising Black children.** Journal of Personality and Social Psychology 106 (4): pp.526-545.

Goldenberg. B.M. (2014**) White Teachers in Urban Classrooms: Embracing Non-White Students' Cultural Capital for Better Teaching and Learning**. Urban Education, Vol 49

Goodwin. M. (2015) **Is it time to ditch the term 'black, Asian and Minority Ethnic' (BAME)?** http://theguardian.com/commentisfree/2015/may/22/black-asian-minority-ethnic-bame-bme

Gordon. L.R. (2006, 2016) **Disciplinary Decadence: Living Thought in Trying Times**. Routledge: London & New York.

Gordon. L. R. (2007) **Problematic People and Epistemic Decolonization. Toward the Postcolonial in African Political Thought.** abahlali.org/files/Gordon-problematic%20people-1%20 (2).pdf.

Graham. L.D. (2013) **Terracotta fertility figurines of prehistoric Eurasian design from modern East Africa.**

Gray. R. (2015) **Are schools still struggling with racism? Teachers more likely to label black students as troublemakers, study finds.** 16th April http://www.dailymail.co.uk/sciencetech/article-3041665

Greenwald. A.G. McGhee. D.R. & Schwartz. J.L.K. (1998) **Measuring Individual Differences in Implicit Cognition: The Implicit Association Test**. Journal of Personality and Social Psychology, 74 (6), pp.1464-1480.

Grollman. E. (2016) **Objectivity and Oppression in Academia**. http://conditionallyaccepted.com

Guinier, L. (2004) **"From Racial Liberalism to Racial Literacy: Brown v Brown of Education and the Interest-Divergence Dilemma."** The Journal of American History 91 (1) pp. 92-118.

Guttenberg Project (2008) **Timaeus.** http://www.gutneberg.org

Haliburton. R.G. (1985) **Dwarf Survivals, and Traditions as to Pygmy Races**. From the Proceedings of the American Association for the Advancement of Science vol, XLIV, 1895.

Hall. S. (1992) **New Ethnicities**. In (eds) Donald. J & Rattansi. A. 'Race', Culture & Difference. SAGE Publications Ltd, London UK.

Hall. S. (1997) **Representation: Cultural Representations and Signifying Practices**. SAGE Publications: Thousand Oaks, California.

Hall, S. (2007) **Preface in P**. Gilroy (2007) Black Britain. A Photographic History. London: Saqi Books.com.

Harewood. D. (2016) **Will Britain ever have a Black Prime Minister?** 16th November http://.bbc.co.uk/news/magazine-37799305

Haslanger. S. (2016) **Objectivity: Epistemic Objectification and Oppression. In Epistemic Injustice and Phenomenology**. The Routledge Handbook of Epistemic Injustice (eds) Kidd. I.J. Medina. J. & Pohlhaus (2017). Taylor & Francis Group

Hassan. N.R. (2013**) Are we using the right "paradigms?" Comparing metaphysical, sociological and conceptual paradigms.** Proceedings of the Nineteenth Americas Conference on Information Systems, Chicago, Illinois, August 15-17, USA.

Hayes. N. (2008) **Teaching matters in early educational practice: The case for a nurturing pedagogy**. Early Education and Development. 19 [3] p.430-44

Hegel. G.W.F. (1807, 1952)) **Phenomenology of Spirit**. Translated by A.V. Miller. Oxford University Press: Oxford, Toronto, Melbourne.

Hegel. G.W. (1910) **The Phenomenology of Mind**. Vol 1. (J.B. Baille, Trans) New York: The Macmillan Company.

Henfield, M.S. & Washington, A.R. (2012) **"I want to do the right thing but what is it?": White Teachers' Experiences with African American Students**. The Journal of Negro Education, Vol 81 (2) pp.148-161.

Henry. R. (MDCCLXXI) A New History of Great Briton from the first invasion of it by Julius Caesar, Volume 1, Cadell Publishers: London, UK.

Henry. P. (2006) **African Phenomenology: Its Philosophical Implications**. Worlds & Knowledges Otherwise, Fall. pp. 1-23.

Hilliard. A.G. III (1978) **Free your mind, return to the source. The African origin of civilization**. Urban Institute for Human Services, San Francisco: USA

Hilliard. A (1985) **The Master Keys to Study Ancient Kemet.** www.youtube.com

Hilliard A. Payton-Stewart L. & Williams L. (1990) **Infusion of African & African-American content in the school Curriculum**: Proceedings of the First National Conference October 1989 Morristown NJ: Aran Press

Hilliard. A. G. III (1992) **Why We Must Pluralize The Curriculum**. Education Leadership, December 1991/January 1992, pp.12-16.

Hilliard. A.G. III (1995) **The Maroon Within Us.** Black Classic Press, Baltimore, MD USA.

Hilliard. A.G. III (2002) **Lefkowitz and the Myth of the Immaculate Conception of Western Civilization: The Myth is Not Out of Africa;** in (eds) Asante. M & Mazama. A. (2002) Egypt Vs Greece and the American Academy: The debate over the birth of civilization African American Images, Chicago, Illinois: USA.

Hilliard. A.G. III (2003**) No Mystery: Closing the achievement gap between Africans and excellence. Young, gifted and black: Promoting high achievement among African American students**, pp.131-165.

Hodgskiss. T. (2015) **What the use of ochre tells us about the capabilities of our African ancestry**. http://theconverstion.com

Hofstede. G. (1980) **Culture's Consequences: International Differences in Work-related Values.** London: Sage Publications.

Holloway. I. (1997) **Basic concepts for qualitative research**. Oxford: Blackwell Science.

Hom, M. (2015) Out **of Africa: retracing human evolution and migration with DNA.** Http://memeburn.com/2015/12/out-of-africa-retracing-human-evolution-and-migrations

Horowitz. D. (2007**) Indoctrination U. The Left's War Against Academic Freedom**. Encounter Books, New York, USA.

Howard.T.C. (2008) **Who really cares? The disenfranchisement of African American males in pre K-12 schools: A critical race theory perspective**. Teachers College Record, 110, pp. 954-985.

Howe. S. (1999) **Afrocentrism: mythical pasts and imagined homes**: Verso, London & New York.

Hoyningen-Huene. P. (1992) The **Interrelations between the Philosophy, History and Sociology of Science in Thomas Kuhn's Theory of Scientific Development**. The British Journal for the Philosophy of Science, 43 (4): pp. 487-501

Houston. M. & Davis. O.I. (2002) **Centering Ourselves. African American Feminist and Womanist Studies of Discourse.** Hampton Press Inc, USA

Humphry. D. & John. G. (1971) Because **They're Black**. Harmondsworth, Penguin.

Husserl. E (1887, 1970) **The Crisis of European Sciences and Transcendental Phenomenology**. Translated by D. Carr Evanston Northwestern University Press.

Hycner. R.H. (1999) **Some guidelines for the phenomenological analysis of interview data**. In (eds) Bryman. A. & Burgess. R.G. Qualitative research (vol 3), pp.143-164. London: SAGE.

Irvine, J.J. (1988) **"An Analysis of the Problem of the Disappearing Black Educator"**. Elementary School Journal 88 (5) pp. 503-514.

Irvine. J.J. (2009) **Teaching Tolerance**. Fall 2009, pp. 40-44. http://www.tolerance.org/magazine/number-36-fall-2009/relevant-beyond-basics

Irvine. J.J. (2010) **Culturally Relevant Pedagogy**. Education Digest, April 2010, pp.57-61 www.eddigest.com

Imhotep. D. (2013) **The First Americans were African: Documented Evidence**. Author House, Bloomington, IN 47403.

Ivimy. J. (1976) **The Sphinx and the Megaliths**. Cox & Wyman Ltd Publishers, London: UK.

James. G.G.M. (1954) **Stolen legacy**. Philosophical Library; New York USA.

James. A & James, A. (2008) **Concepts of Childhood Studies**. UK Sage

John. G. (1976) **The New Black Presence in Britain**. London: British Council of Churches

John. G. (2005) **Parental and Community Involvement in Education: Time to get the balance right**. In (ed) Richardson. B. Tell It Like It Is: How Our Schools Fail Black Children. Book mark Publications; Trentham Books, London

Johnson. U. (2013) **Psycho-Academic Holocaust: The Special Education & ADHD Wars Against Black Boys**. Pan-Africanism Publishing

Johnson, U. (2015) **Out of Darkness.** Documentary produced by Amadeuz Christ: outofdarknessfilm.com

Jones. C. (1958) **The West Indian Gazette.** Lambeth, London.

Jones. D. (1990) **Culture Bandits**. Hikeka Press, first edition.

Kamene. K (2019) **Spirituality Before Religions: Spirituality is unseen science...Science is seen spirituality.** www.kabakamene.com

Kang. J. Bennett. M. Carbado. D. Casey. P. Dasgupta. N. & Faigman. D. (2012) **Implicit Bias in the Courtroom.** UCLA Law Review, 59 (5), pp.1124-1186.

Karenga. M. (2003) **Afrocentricity and Multicultural Education: Concept, Challenge and Contribution.** In (ed) Mazama. A (2003) The Afrocentric Paradigm, pp. 73-94; Africa World Press, Trenton NJ, USA

Karenga. M. (2006b) Maat, **the moral ideal of ancient Egypt: A study in classical African ethics**. New York, NY: Routledge.

.

King. J (2003) **'Lochy' Names and Adoman's Nigra Dea**. www.snsbi.org.uk

King. J.E. (2004) **Culture-centered knowledge: Black studies, curriculum transformation, and social action.** In J. A. Banks & C. A. McGee Banks (eds), *Handbook of research on multicultural education* (2nd ed), pp. 349-378. Jossey-Bass: USA.

King. J.E. (2015**) Dysconscious racism, Afrocentric praxis and education for human freedom: Through the years I keep on toiling.** The selected works of Joyce E. King, Routledge: USA.

King. J.E. & Swartz. E.E. (2018) **Heritage Knowledge in the Curriculum.** Routledge, New York and London.

Koutonin. M. (2016) **Story of cities #5: Benin City, the mighty medieval capital now lost without trace.** 18th March http://www.theguardian.com

Kress. G. (2003**) Literacy in the New Media Age.** London: Routledge.

Kuhn. T. (2012) **The Structure of Scientific Revolutions.** University of Chicago Press: Chicago USA.

Kunjufu. J. (1984) Countering **the conspiracy to Destroy Black Boys, Vol I** .African American Images, Chicago Illinois.

Kunjufu. J. (1986) **Countering the Conspiracy to Destroy Black Boys, Vol II** African American Images, Chicago, Illinois.

Kunjufu. J (1990) **Countering the Conspiracy to Destroy Black Boys, Vol III** African America Images, Chicago, Illinois.

Kush. I.K (2000) **Enoch the Ethiopian.** A & B Publishers, Brooklyn, New York.

Kush. I.K. (2012**) In Defense of Stolen Legacy. The African Origins of Western Civilization and Greek Philosophy and the African Contributions to World Progress and Civilization.** EWorld publishing, Buffalo New York USA.

Kuyk. B.M. (2003) **African Voices in the African American Heritage.** Indiana University Press. Bloomington & Indianapolis, USA.

Ladson-Billings, G. J. (2005) **"Is the Team All Right? Diversity and Teacher Education".** Journal of Teacher Education, 56 (3) pp.47-68.

Ladson-Billings. G.J. (2009) **The Dream Keepers: Successful Teachers of African American Children.** Jossey-Bass Books, San Francisco, CA.

Ladson-Billings. G.J. (2011) **Boyz to Men? Teaching to restore Black boys' childhood.** Race, Ethnicity and Childhood, 14, pp.7-15.

Laude. J. (1973) **African Art of the Dogon. The Myths of the Cliff Dwellers.** Viking press: New York, USA

Lauwers.H. (2013) **Phenomenological research in educational sciences or learning how to cope with ambiguity**. Childhood & Society Research Centre, Brussels, Belgium.

Leakey. L.S. (1980) **Adam's Ancestors the Evolution of Man and his Culture**. Peter Smith Publishers.

Lederach. J.P. (1995) **Preparing for Peace: Conflict transformation across cultures.** Syracuse, NY: Syracuse University Press.

Lee. E. S. (2014) **Living Alterities: Phenomenology. Embodiment. And Race.** State University of New York Press, Albany

Lefkowitz. M. (1996) **Not Out of Africa**. Basic Books: New York USA.

Leonardo, Z. (2002) "**The Souls of White Folk: Critical Pedagogy, Whiteness Studies and Globalisation Discourse**" Race Ethnicity & Education vol 5 (1) pp. 29-50.

Leonardo. Z. (2005). **Critical Pedagogy and Race**. Blackwell Publishing: Victoria, Australia.

Lemon. G.W. (1783) **English Etymology; Or, A Derivative Dictionary of the English and Globalisation Discourse**" Race Ethnicity & Education vol 5 (1) pp. 29-50.**Language in two Alphabets.** Printed for G. Robinson in Pater-Noster Row: London.

Levi, J.B. (2012) **The Intellectual Warfare of Dr Jacob H. Carruthers and the Battle for Ancient Nubia as a Foundational Paradigm in Africana Studies:**

Lewis. B. (1998) **The Multiple Identities of the Middle East**: Weidenfeld and Nicolson: London UK.

Lichtheim. M. (1975) **Ancient Egyptian Literature, Volume I**. University of California Press, Berkeley, CA, USA.

List. R. N. (1999) Merlin's Secret. **The African Near Eastern Presence in the Ancient British Isles.** University press of America.

Loi. M. Del Savio. L. & Stupka. E. (2013) **Social Epigenetics and Equality of Opportunity**. Public Health Ethics, July: 6 (2): pp .142-153.

Loring Brace, C. (2007) **'Race' is a four letter word. The Genesis of the Concept**. Oxford University Press.

Luke. D (1990) **African Presence in the Early History of the British Isles and Scandinavia.** In (Ed) African Presence in Early Europe. Ivan Van Sertima, Journal of African Civilizations LTD: Published by Rutgers- The State University, New Jersey USA.

Maat. S.R.E.K & Carroll. K.K. (2012) **African-Centered Theory and Methodology in Africana Studies: An Introduction.** The Journal of Pan African Studies, vol 5 (4), June, pp.1-11.

Mac an Ghaill, M. (1988) **Young, Gifted and Black: Student-teacher relations in the schooling of black youth**. Milton Keynes, Open University Press.

Mackenzie. D. A. (1917) **Myths of Crete & Pre-Hellenic Europe.** eBook: https://www.kobo.com

MacRichie. D. (1893) **Fians, Fairies and Picts**. Kegan Paul, Trench, Trubner & Co Ltd, London: UK.

Mahendran. D. (2007) **The Facticity of Blackness. A Non-conceptual approach to the study of Race and Racism in Fanon's and Merleau-Ponty's Phenomenology**. Human Architecture: Journal of the Sociology of Self-Knowledge. Vol 5 (3), pp. 191-204.

Makin. L. & Whiteman. P. (2006) **Young children as active participants in the investigation of teaching and learning**. European Early Childhood Education Research Journal. 14 [1] p.33-41

Manias. C. (2012) **Our Iberian Forefathers: The Deep Past and Racial Stratification of British Civilization**. Journal of British Studies 51 (October), pp 910-935.

Masterman. M. (1970) **The nature of a paradigm in criticism and the growth of knowledge: International colloquium in the philosophy of science** (B*edford college*, 1965), I. Lakatos and A. Musgrave (eds) London: Cambridge University Press, pp. 59-89.

Matthews. J. (1999). **The Art of Childhood and Adolescence: The Construction of Meaning**. London: Falmer Press.

Mayhew. R. (2005) **Ayn Rand Answers. The Best of Her Q & A**. pp 102-104: NAL Trade.

Mazama. A. (2003**) The Afrocentric Paradigm**. Africa World Press, UK edition.

McAdamis. S. 2001. **Teachers tailor their instruction to meet a variety of students' needs**. Journal of Staff Development 22 [2] p. 1-5

McGowan. M. (2017) **Schools are a microcosm of society: The quest to close Australia's education gap.** http://www.theguardian.com/australia-news/2017/sep/27

McIntyre, A. (1997) **Making meaning of Whiteness: Exploring racial identity with White teachers**. New York: State University of New York.

McNiff. J. & Whitehead. J. (2000) **Action Research in Organisations**. Routledge London: New York

Merleau-Ponty. M. (1968) **The Visible and the Invisible.** (trans by Lingis. A.) Northwestern University Press

Merleau-Ponty. M. (2002) **Phenomenology of perception** (trans by Smith. C) London: Routledge Classics.

Mfundishi. J. (2016) **The Spiritual Warriors are Healers**. Charles Child Publishing, Indiana, USA.

Miller. K. (1908) **Race adjustment: Essays on the Negro in America**. New York: Neale.

Miller M.D (2009) **Ancient Egyptian Sacred Geometry: Designing Your Home With Sacred Geometry And Other Useful Secrets Of Harmonic Resonance For Greater Peace Of Mind, Health And Wellbeing**. es.scribd.com

Mills. C.W. (1997) **The racial contract**. Cornel University Press: New York, USA

Milner, H.R. (2011) **Culturally relevant pedagogy in a diverse urban classroom**. Urban Review, 43 (1) pp. 66-89.

Monges. M.M.K.R. (1997**) Kush: The Jewel of Nubia. Reconnecting the root system of African Civilization.** Africa World Press Inc, Trenton NJ, USA.

Morakinyo. O (2016) Notion **of 'African' as a strategic ideological epistemic position in African philosophy.** Phronimon, vol 17 (2) pp .1-10.

Morris. E.F. (2011) **Paddle Dolls and Performance**. Journal of the American Research Center in Egypt, vol 47, pp 71-103.

Munro. R. (1899) **Prehistoric Scotland and its place in European Civilization**. William Blackwood & Sons; Edinburgh and London.

Myers. J. M. (2012) **The Scholarship of Cedric J. Robinson: Methodological Considerations for Africana Studies.** The Journal of Pan African Studies, vol 5 (4) June, pp. 46-82.

Namono. C. (2012) **Dumbbells and circles: Symbolism of Pygmy rock art of Uganda**. Journal of Social Archaeology 12 (3) pp 404-425.

Nichols. E .J. (1986) **Cultural Foundations for Teaching Black Children in Teaching Mathematics volume 1: Culture, Motivation, History and Classroom Management** (ed) O.M.T. Ratteray; Institute for Independent Education, Washington, D.C. USA.

Nichols. E. J. (2018) **Dr Edwin Nichols on Dichotomous Logic and Colorism**. April 10th http://www.youtube.com

Nieto, S. (2002**) Language, Culture, and Teaching: Critical Perspectives for a New Century**. NJ Lawrence Erlbaum Associates.

Nieto. S. (2004) **Affirming Diversity: The Sociopolitical Context of Multicultural Education**. New York: Longman.
.

Nissim-Sabat. M. (2008) **Coming Out of the Closet: Phenomenology, African Studies, and Human Liberation**. Radical Philosophy Review, vol 11 (2), pp. 159-173.

Nkulu-N'Sengha. M. (2005) **African epistemology.** In M. K. Asante & A. Mazama (Eds) Encyclopaedia of Black Studies, pp. 39-44. SAGE: Thousand Oaks, CA, USA.

Nobles. W. (2006) **Seeking the Sakhu: Foundational Writings for an African Psychology**. Third World Press Foundation, Chicago USA.

Nobles. W. (2010) **The Infusion of African and African-American Content: A question of Content and Intent- The role of Culture in Education**. www.nuatc.org/articles/pdf/Nobles_article.pdf

Nobles, W. (2015) **The Island of Memes: Haiti's Unfinished Revolution.** Inprint Editions, Black Classic Press.

Nobles. W. (2017). **Reclaiming Education for African People**. http://www.youtube.com

Nobles. W. (2017) **Empowering African People**. http://www.youtube.com

Nosek. B.A. Smith. F.L. Hansen.J.J. Devos.T. Linder. N.M. Ranganath. K.A. (2007). **Pervasiveness and Correlates of Implicit Attitudes and Stereotypes.** European Review of Social Psychology, 18, pp. 36-88.

Obenga. T. (1992) **Ancient Egypt and Black Africa**. Karnak House, London: UK.

Obenga, T. (1995**) La Geometrie Egyptienne: Contribution de L'Afrique antique a la Mathematique mondiale:** Editions L' Harmattan; Kheprai.

Obenga. T. (2004) **African Philosophy: The Pharonic Period 2780-330 BC**. Per Ankh Publishing, Senegal: Africa.

Obenga. T. (2015) **African Philosophy**. Brawtley Press.

Obenga. T. (2016) **the African Origin of So-Called Greek Education and Philosophy**. November 6th http://www.youtube.com

Odwirafo (2015) Ancestral Roots of Nanasom in Khanit/Keneset and Kamit (Ancient Nubia and Egypt). http://www/odwirafo.com/nanasom.html

Ogbu. J.U. (2004**) Collective Identity and Burden of "Acting White" in Black History, Community, and Education.** The Urban Review, Vol 36 (1) March, pp.1-35.

Olusoga, D. (2015) **Black History Month needs a rethink: it's time to ditch the heroes**. 9th October http://www.theguardian.com

Okonofua. J. & Eberhardt. J. L (2015) **Two Strikes: Race and Disciplining of Young Students.** Psychological Science, pp.1-8

Olusoga, D. (2015) **Black History Month needs a rethink: it's time to ditch the heroes**. 9th October http://www.theguardian.com

Osaze .J. (2016) **Seven little white lies: the conspiracy to destroy the Black self image**. African Genesis Institute Press, Pennsylvania USA

Outlaw, L. T. (1996) **On Race and Philosophy**. Routledge: New York.

Pacheco. E.V. & Ortiz. T.A. (2004) **The Crocodile and the Cosmos: Itzamkanac, the place of the Alligator's home**. www.famsi.org.reports

Padmore. G. (1931) **The Life and Struggles of Negro Toilers**. Red International of Labour of Unions Magazine for the International Trade Union Committee of Negro Workers.

Padmore, G. (1965-1988) **George Padmore Institute Archive Catalogue**. http://www.georgepadmoreinstitute.org/archive/collection/black-education-movement.uk

Padmore. G. (1969) **How Britain Rules Africa**. Negro University Press.

Padmore. G. (1971) **Pan-Africanism or Communism? The Coming Struggle for Africa**. Doubleday publishing.

Pennington, J.L. Brock, C.H. & Ndura, E (2012) **Unravelling the threads of White teachers' conceptions of caring: Repositioning White privilege.** Urban Education, 47,

Petre. M. & Rugg. G. (2004) **The Unwritten Rules of PhD Research**. Open University Press. McGraw-Hill Education, Berkshire, UK.

Perrenoud. P. (1998) **From formative evaluation to a controlled regulation of learning processes. Towards a wider conceptual field**. Assessment in Education 5 (1) pp. 85-102.

Peters. M. (2015) **Why is my curriculum white?** Educational Philosophy and Theory, 47, pp 641-646

Poe. R. (1997) **Black Spark White Fire. Did African Explorers Civilize Ancient Europe?** Prima Publishing, California: USA.

Plato. **Laws, Book 7** http://www/perseus.tufts.edu

Preszler. R.W. (2009) **Replacing Lecture with Peer-led Workshops Improves Student Learning**. CBE Life Sciences Education, Fall 2009; 8 (3) pp. 182-192.

Rachlinski. J.J. Johnson, S.L. Wistrich, A. J. & Guthrie. C. (2009) **Does Unconscious Racial Bias Affect Trial Judges**? Notre Dame Law Review, 84, (3) pp. 1195-1246.

Rajagopal. K. (2011) **Create Success! Unlocking the Potential of Urban Students**. Association for Supervision & Curriculum Development.

Rand. A & Branden. N. (1962) Counterfeit **Individualism**. Objectivist Newsletter, Vol 1 (4), p.13

Rand. A & Schwartz. P. (1999) Return **of the Primitive: The Anti-Industrial Revolution**. Meridian: Penguin Group: New York, USA.

Rashidi. R. (2011) Black Star. The African Presence in Early Europe. Books of Africa Limited, London UK.

Ray. M. (1994) **The Richness of Phenomenology: Philosophic, Theoretic and Methodologic Concerns.** In (ed) Morse. J.M. Critical Issues in Qualitative Research Methods. Thousand Oaks: SAGE.

Rawlinson. G. (1880) **History of Herodotus. In Four Volumes- Vol II**. John Murray, Albemarle Street. London UK.

Reid. P. (2014) **At last, a home for black history**. 23rd July

Resnick. B. (2017) **White fear of demographic change is a powerful psychological force.** January, 28th http://www.vox.com

Reuters (2015) **Revealed: the terrifying 9ft- long crocodile that walked upright**. 20th March http://www.theguardian.com

Rhamie. J. (2007) **Eagles who soar: How black learners find the path to success**. Stoke on Trent, Trentham Books.

Rice-Holmes. T. (1907) **Ancient Britain and the Invasions of Julius Caesar**. Oxford at the Clarendon Press.

Richards. D. (1989) **Toward the Demystification of Objectivity,** in Imhotep, Journal of Afrocentric Thought, vol 1 (1) Department of African American Studies, Temple University, pp. 23-34.

Ripley. W.Z. (1899) **The Races of Europe: A Sociological Study**. D. Appleton & Company Publishers; New York: USA.

Roger. A.K. (1908) **A Student's History of Philosophy**. The Macmillan Company: London

Rogers. J.A. (1952/1980) **Nature Knows no Color- Line**. Wesleyan University Press: USA.

Rogers. J.A. (1968) **Sex and Race. Negro-Caucasian Mixing in All Ages and All Lands. Volume I: The Old World**. Wesleyan University Press, USA.

Rosenthal. R. & Jacobson. L. (1968) **Pygmalion in the Classroom.** The Urban review, September vol (1) pp.16-20.

Roundtree. C. (2017) **Parents outraged after fifth grade class has a mock slave auction and a black student was sold to bidding white students**. 21st March.

Saint-Aubin. A. (1994) **Testeria: the dis-ease of black men in white supremacist, patriarchal culture.** Callaloo, vol 17, (4), pp. 1054-1073.

Sammes. A. (1675) **Britannia Antiqua Illustrata: or the Antiquities of Ancient Britain, Derived from the Phoenicians.** Printed by The Roycroft: London

Sanford. E. M. (1938) **The Mediterranean World in Ancient Times**. The Ronald Press Company: New York

Scheinfeldt. L. B. Soi. S. & Tishkoff. S. A. (2010) **Working toward a synthesis of archaeological, linguistic, and genetic data for inferring African population history**. Proceedings of the National Academy of Sciences of the United States of America. May 11, Vol 107 (2) pp. 8931-8938.

Schlesinger. A. M. Jr (1992) **The disuniting of America: Reflections on a multicultural society**. WW. Norton & Company: New York USA.

Shank, R.A. (2016) **Contexts that inform racial awareness and affect teaching practice: A study of White bilingual teachers**.
http://digital.lib.washington.edu/.../shank_washington_0250E_16505.pdf

Sharkey. J. (1975) **Celtic Mysteries**. Thames & Hudson: London, UK.

Shockley. K. (2008) **The Miseducation of Black Children**. African American Images: Chicago

Simpson. W. (1973) **The Literature of Ancient Egypt.** Yale University Press, New Haven, Connecticut, USA.

Snowden. F.M. (1983**) Before Color Prejudice**. The Ancient View of Blacks. Harvard University Press, USA.

Sollas. W.J. (1911) **Ancient Hunters and their Modern Representatives**. MacMillan & Co, LTD, London: UK

South African Architectural Record (1950), February, volume 35 (2), pp. 1-23

Spretnak. C. (2011) **Anatomy of a Backlash: Concerning the Work of Marija Gimbutas.** Journal of Archaeomythology, 7, x-xx, pp 1-27.

Straiton. E.V. (1927) Celestial Ship of the North. Kessinger Legacy Reprints.

Strand. S. (2015) **Ethnicity, deprivation and educational achievement at age 16 in England: trends over time. Annex to compendium of evidence on ethnic minority resilience to the effects of deprivation on attainment.** June 2015, Department for Education

Strong. R. (1996) The Story of Britain. A People's History. Plimico, Random House: London, UK.

Squire. C. (1910) Celtic Myth & Legend, Poetry & Romance. The Gresham Publishing Company, London: UK.

Sullivan. S. & Tuana. N. (2007) **Race and Epistemologies of Ignorance**. State University of New York Press, Albany, USA.

Taylor. J.A. (2007) **Consciousness in Black: A Historical look at the Phenomenology of W.E.B Dubois and Franz Fanon**. Graduate College of Bowling Green State University, USA.

Temple. R. (2000) The Crystal Sun. Rediscovering a Lost Technology of the Ancient World. Century-Random House Group Limited, London, UK.

Thorndike, R.L. (1968) **Review of the book Pygmalion in the classroom**. American Educational Research Journal. Vol 5 (4) pp. 708-711.

Throop. J.C. & Murphy. K.M. (2002**) Bourdieu and Phenomenology: A critical assessment.** Anthropological Theory, Vol 2 (2), pp.185-207.

Tillotson. M.T. (2011) **Retrospective Analysis: The Movement Against African-Centered Thought**. The Journal of Pan African Studies, vol 4 (3), March, pp. 155-174.

Tomlinson. S. (1989) Ethnicity **and Educational Achievement in Britain.** In L. Eldering & J. Kloprogge (Eds). Different cultures, same school: Ethnic minority children in Europe, pp. 15-37. Amsterdam: Sewts & Zeitlinger.

Tomlinson. C.A. (2001) **Differentiated instruction in the regular classroom: What does it mean? How does it look**? Understanding Our Gifted. 14 [1] p.3-6

Treisman .U. (1992) Studying **Students studying Calculus: A look at the Lives of Minority Mathematics Students in College.** The College Mathematics Journal, 23, pp. 363-372.

T'Shaka. O. (2001) **A Return to the Afrikan Mother Principle of Male and Female Equality.** http://www.raceandhistory.com

Tuffour. I. (2017) **A Critical Overview of Interpretative Phenomenological Analysis: A Contemporary Qualitative Research Approach.** Journal of Healthcare Communications. Vol 2 (4), pp. 1-5.

Turner. W. (1903) **History of Philosophy**. Ginn & Company: Boston & London.
Turner. J. (1971) **Black Studies and a Black Philosophy of Education**. *Imani* (August-September, pp.12-17.

Turner. J. (1984) Africana **Studies and Epistemology: A Discourse in the**

Turner. J. (2014) **Theoretical and Research Issues in African Studies**. Diasporic Africa Press, NY, USA.

Turner. J. (2016) Discourse **on African Studies. James Turner and Paradigms of Knowledge** (ed) Scot Brown. Diasporic Africa press Inc, New York.

UNESCO (1978) **Declaration on Race and Racial Prejudice**, 27th November 1978. www.unesco.org

Valentine. P. (2016) **Holistic Health Conference** ft Lalia Afrika and Dr Valentine. http://youtube.com

Van Manen. M. (1990) **Researching Lived Experience. Human Science for an Action Sensitive Pedagogy.** State University of New York Press (SUNY Series).

Van Sertima. I (1995) **Egypt: Child of Africa**. Transaction Publishers: New Brunswick, USA & London.

Walker. D. (1829/1965) **David Walker's appeal**. C.M. Wiltse (ed), Hill and Wang, New York, USA.

Walker. B (1983) **The Women's Encyclopedia of Myths and Secrets.** Harper & Row Publishers, San Francisco: USA

Walker. C. E. (2001) **Can't go home again: An argument about Afrocentrism**. Oxford University Press.

Weale. S. (2017) **East London primary school head apologises for slave dress letter.** 17th October http://www.theguardian.com/education

Weiler. N. (2017) **Cultural Differences may leave their mark on DNA. Epigenetic signatures distinguishing Mexican and Puerto Rican children cannot be explained by Genetic Ancestry alone.** http://www.ucsf.edu.news/2017/405466

Williams. C. J. (1987) **The Destruction of Black Civilization. Great Issues of a Race from 4500B.C to 2000** A.D. Third World Press: US.

Williams. W. (1992) **The Historical Origin of Christianity.** Maathian Press, Chicago, Illinois, USA.

Williams. R. L. (2008) **History of the Association of Black Psychologists**. Author House, Bloomington, IN, USA.

Wilson. A. N. (1991) **Awakening the Natural Genius of Black Children**. Afrikan World InfoSystems, New York, USA.

Wilson. A. N. (1993) **The Falsification of Afrikan Consciousness. Eurocentric History, Psychiatry and the Politics of White Supremacy**. Afrikan World InfoSystems; New York.

Winters. C. A. (2013) **A Short World History of Black People in Ancient Times**. Create Space Independent Publishing Platform- Amazon Company.

Wells. I. B. (1892) **Southern horrors: Lynch law in all its phases**. New York: The New York Age Print.

Wheelwright. P. (1988) **The Presocratics**. MacMillan Publishing Company; New York USA.

Wikipedia (2018) **Objectivism's rejection of the primitive**, 9th August. http://en.wikipedia.org

Williams. C. J. (1987) **The Destruction of Black Civilization. Great Issues of a Race from 4500B.C to 2000** A.D. Third World Press: US.

Willoughby. P. R. (2007) **The Evolution of Modern Humans in Africa: A Comprehensive Guide**. AltaMira Press.

Wong. B. (2015) **A blessing with a curse: Model minority ethnic students and the construction of educational success**. Oxford Review of Education 41 (6); pp. 730-746.

Woodson. C. G. (1919a) **The education of the negro prior to 1861: A history of the education of the Colored people of the United States from the beginning of slavery to the Civil War**. G.P. Putnam's Sons: New York & London.

Woodson. C.G. (1919b) **Negro life and history as presented in the schools**. The Journal of Negro History, 4, pp. 273-280.

Woodson. C. G. (1933/2010) **The mis-education of the Negro**. Seven Treasures Publications, USA.

Wright. C. (1988) **School process: An ethnographic study**. In M.Woodhead & A.McGrath (Eds). Family, school and society (pp. 197-214). Buckingham, UK, Open University Press.

Wright. C. (1992) **Race Relations in the primary school**. London: David Fulton

Wright. B. L. & Counsell. S. L. (2018) **The Brilliance of Black Boys. Cultivating School Success in the Early Grades.** Teachers College Press. Columbia University, New York & London.

Wright. C. Maylor. U. & Becker. S. (2016) **Young black males: resilience and the use of capital to transform school 'failure'.** Critical Studies in Education. DOI; 10.1080/17508487.2016.1117005.

Wynter. S. (2006) **On how we mistook the map for the territory, and re-imprisoned ourselves in our unbearable wrongness of being: Black studies toward the human project.** In L.R.Gordon & J.A. Gordon (eds), *Not only the master's tools: African American studies in theory and practice* (pp.107-169). Paradigm Publishers; USA.

Yancy. G. (2004) **What White looks Like. African-American Philosophers On The Whiteness Question**. Routledge. New York. London

Yancy. G. (2014) **White Gazes: What It Feels Like to Be an Essence**. In (ed) Lee. E.S. (2014) living Alterities. Phenomenology, Embodiment, and Race. State University of New York Press, Albany, USA.

Yehudah. M. Z (2015) Distinguishing **Afrocentric Inquiry from Pop Culture Afrocentrism**. Journal of Black Studies, Vol 46 (6) pp. 551-563.

Young. Y. (2016) **Teachers' implicit bias against black students starts in preschool, study finds**. 4th October: http://www.theguardian.com

Zeller. E. (1896) **Outlines of the History of Greek Philosophy**. Longmans, Green, & Co: London

Zulu. I. M. (2012) **The Ancient Kemetic Roots of Library and Information Science**. The Journal of Pan African Studies, vol5 (1), March, pp.1-26.

Index

Episodes, p. 4; episodic history p. 9, 13, 90, 106.
Epoisteme: p.57.
Ethics/ethical: p.35.
Ethnicity: p.23, 25, 29; ethnic underachievement p.30, 32; mixed ethnicities p.9, 12, 32.
Etymology: definition of p.7, 8, 26, 54, 87, 100; etymological origin p.52; etymological source of concepts p. 102.
Euclid: p. 63.
Eurocentric, p 13, 41,49, 66; Eurocentric paradigm p. 9, 85, 89, 104; dominance of Eurocentrism p. 41, 49; European constructs p. 12; European hegemony p. 3; Euro-American: p.45.
Evolution: p.13; polygenetic theory p. 13; monogenetic theory p.13.

F
Fanon, Franz: p.20, 21, 22, 27.
Feminine Principle: Great Mother p.104.
Fertility: p.85.
Formative: p.7, 9, 10, 16.
Framework: p. 43; conceptual & theoretical framework p. 5, 8, 9, reconceptualized teaching framework p. 5.

G
General Certificate of Secondary Education [GCSE]: p.30; GCSE performance data p.30; under-achievement p.30.
Genesis of Geometry: p. 6, 8, 51, 53, 75, 103; Black genesis of geometry p.8,
Genetics: p. 12, 13, 25.
Geographical: p.56,
Geology: p. 69, 70.
Geometry: p. 6, 55, 56, 85, 90; triangles p. 84-85; geometrical representation p. 85, 86, 103.
Global connections and triangles: p.8.
Global majority: p.123.

Guided group: formative pedagogy p. 7, 54, 55; impact of p. 70.

H

Hathor [Great Mother]: p.102, 104.
Hegel: Hegelian thesis: p. 17, 18, 45, 66.
Hegemony: p.47.
Heku Ptah: p.55.
History: p.13, 37, 39, 48, 58, 79, 91,101; distortion of history p.8, damaged histories p. 11,12,14, 91; reclamation of cultural heritage p 14, 44; episodic history p. 9,13, 90,106; misleading historical chronology p. 9, 64,90; misinterpretations of history p.11, 90; psycho-history p.13,14; socio-historical reality p.20; 25; historiography: p. 57, 80, 81.
Homo sapiens: p.13.
Hydronomy [the study of names of bodies of water and the origins of those names through history] p.104
Hypotenuse: p. 60, 62-64.

I

Imhotep: p. 74.

Inclusion p. 9, 10; inclusive schooling environment p. 6; modelling inclusive teaching/pedagogy p. 33.

Income: p.34.

Indigenous people: Ireland p. 94; Firbolgs p. 94; Tuatha de Danaan p. 94; Nemedians p.94; Parthalonians p. 94; Fomarians p. 94; people of darkness p. 94; Anu p.95.

Integration: p.5, 6, 53.

IQ testing: p. 35, 36.

K

Kells [Book of]: p.99.

Kemet/Kemites: p. 3, 15, 44, 62, 63, 64, 74, 78, 88, 89, 100; Kemetic mathematics p. 9, 62, 85, 88; Kemetic teaching: p. 54, 72; Kemitic art p.85; Kemetic cord p.86, 88; Kemetic ancestors p.9.

Kemtiou: p.55.

Knowledge: p.57.

L

Language: p. 26, 27, 66, 67; Language and Etymology of First World People p.6.

Learning: learning behaviours p.5, 55, 107; learner identities p.9, 14; learner empowerment p. 107; 'ideal' learner p. 39; diverse learners, p. 4; learning space p.66, 75; learning styles p.34.

Lens: p.5.

M

Maafa: p.22.

Ma'atian: p.89.

Magnet: p. 71, 72, 86.

Map: p.56.

Mathematics: p. 6, 9,10, 34, 35, 62, 64, 89, 104, 105; numbers p. 62; operational relationships p. 66; multiplication p. 62, 65; squaring p.8, 62, 65; cultural groups studying mathematics p.34; science p.6.

Measurement: Order and arrangement: p.6, 7.

Media: p.67.

Media res: p.92.

Melanin: definition of p.3,39, 80, 94; melanocyte p. 3, 4; Melanated Global Majority [MGM] p. 4,.28, 32, 34,50; stereotypical views of p.32.

Mda Ntr: p.54.

Methodology: definition of tools p. 3, 17, 32, 42, 48, 51, 52, 76, 106.

Merleau-Ponty: p. 21, 22.

Minority: p.25, 26, 27; ethnic minority students' failure p. 32, 34; Minority Group Status p. 35, 90; model minority p.25.

Moral: moral behavior: p. 72.

Motivation: p. 5, 6, 30, 34, 67, 107.

Multimodality p.5, 10, 58,67, 70, 80; language, print, images, graphics, gesture, sound & movement p. 59; synchronous modes p. 67; judicious use of visuals p. 67.

Myths: p. 4, 11, 12, 28, 32.

Reconceptualised Pedagogical programme: p.35;

Red ochre: p.91, 92.

Reframed Curriculum Units of Change p. 5,6, 9,10, 39, 43, 50, 51, 58, 59; definition of p. 7, 9.

Reframing: definition of p. 7; reframed learner-centred approach, p. 4.

Regression: p. 29.

Resistance: p.4, 36.

Rhind Mathematical Papyrus: p. 9.

S

Scaffolding: p. 64.

Schooling: p.3, 11, 13, 27, 28, 29, 31, 36; socio-political dimensions p. 11, 27; microcosm of society p. 28.

Scotland: p.99; carved Pictish stone p.99, 100; 'dumbbells' – Ross-shire, Dumfries & Galloway, p.100; East Dunbartonshire p.100.

Seba: p.54, 56.

Seeking the sakhu: knowing oneself p.15, 19.

Self: p.33; self-regulation [learner autonomy] p.9.

Silures: p. 91.

Socialisation: p.38; the process of socialization p. 18.

Socio-cultural domain: p.11, 15, 19.

Socio-emotional needs: p.38.

Socrates: p.85.

Sophos: p.54.

Squaring numbers and their historical origins: p.8.

Student: student as deficit model p. 27, 28; racialized experiences of black students in the schooling system p.29, 39; objects of measurement/analysis p. 9, 29; student empowerment p.5, 9; 'coloured' students p.31, 36; student as troublemaker p.33; student-centred teaching p.55, 75, 107.

Subjects: subjects with agency: p.44; subject domains p. 6, 11, 72; physics p. 67, 69, 70, 75.

T

Tal-y-llyn: plaque p. 95- 97.

Taxonomy: p. 12; 'wastebasket' taxonomy p.12.

Teaching: teaching programme p. 6, 35, 51; teaching resources p. 7; formative teaching & learning p 5, 54; teaching sessions p. 6, 7, 8, 9, 53, 88 ; modelling teaching p. 6,8; pre-service teaching programmes p. 9, 106; culturally responsive teaching p. 31, 33, 34, ; teacher-effect research p. 35; white teaching percentage p.66; professional development support p.6, 9.

Teleology: p. 43, 50.

The Black Escalating Effect: p.36.

The Doulton Report [1969]: p. 31.

The Maafa: p.22.

The Pygmalion Effect: p. 35, 36.

The Sesh: p. 47.

The University of Liverpool: p.31.

Transmission: p, 11, 59, 81.

Transaction: p.55, 59.

Transformational: p. 38, 43.

Notes on Authors

Dr Marie Charles

Dr Marie Charles initially taught as a primary class teacher before moving into pedagogical research and teacher education. With a career spanning over 30 years, she has taught across the range from young children to adults in Higher Education Institutions in the UK, USA (North Carolina, California, New York), United Arab Emirates, Russia, Saudi Arabia, Thailand and Canada. Dr Charles is a specialist in modelling in classroom situations the range of formative teaching methodologies including guided group working, the use of differentiation and the development of learner autonomy.

Dr Charles has published extensively in international peer reviewed journals and is the co-author of a trilogy of research-based books on formative teaching based on multimodalities and multiliteracies. Dr Charles is also the Director of the Many Faces in Teaching [MFIT] organisation which gathers and publishes research-based programmes to empower the learner and facilitator/teacher.

Dr Charles has a doctorate in Cultural Studies and Humanities with a special focus on curriculum writing and reconceptualised a curriculum programme called 'Reframed Units of Change' (RUoCs) in 2019 and was published in the Journal of Black Studies. She has also designed, developed and delivered workshops for the UK Teachers' Unions on the themes of racial diversity, systems of classification and power; the school-to-prison-pipeline and myth making to myth-breaking all within a socio-cultural - historical framework.

Dr Charles has developed a teaching programme around the Genesis of Geometry which is linked to our African origins and the subsequent migrations out of Africa, with a focus on the material culture that our ancestors, conceived, developed and sustained over many millennia. MFIT exists to hear the agency of those who are reacting and responding in such a way; that we want them to know that these structures are always contingent, tentative, provisional, and therefore, subject to transformation.

Professor Bill Boyle

Professor Boyle has had a 45 year career in transforming sustainable education for stakeholders across the range of national and international. Initially as a classroom teacher, school leader and Local Authority Adviser; then, since 1989, as the Director of an internationally reputed Centre for Formative Assessment Studies and technical Director/Senior Adviser on system development projects for the leading global education development agencies.

From 1989 until January 2014, Professor Bill Boyle was Professor of Education, the Chair of Educational Assessment and the founding Director of the Centre for Formative Assessment Studies (CFAS) in the School of Education, University of Manchester (UK). Professor Boyle is currently supplying international education system analysis and design for curriculum, teaching, learning and assessment.

Professor Boyle was co-founder of the Centre for Formative Assessment Studies at the University of Manchester's School of Education in 1989. CFAS was the oldest established Centre for research and development in formative assessment in the UK. During his time as Director of CFAS, Professor Boyle developed a range of Masters' programmes in Teaching, Learning and Assessment and worked alongside thousands of schools in England as Director of the UK government's Qualifications and Curriculum Authority's [QCA] School Sampling Project and Monitoring Curriculum and Assessment longitudinal research projects [1996-2007]. He also extended CFAS's work into international formative assessment consultancy undertaking design and development work with over 40 countries from Early Years to Higher Education phases.

Professor Boyle worked with the UK government's national assessment team from 1989 until 2009, developing and critically evaluating assessment tasks/items for primary and secondary school pupils. He was Director of the national consultation with schools for the National Curriculum 2000 revisions and supplied longitudinal large-scale assessment system evidence for the UK government's Parliamentary Select Committee Report on the National Curriculum and its Assessment (2008-9).

Printed in Great Britain
by Amazon

48074247R00084